FAVORITE BRAND NAME™

Made | Simple™

Chinese

Publications International, Ltd.

Favorite Brand Name Recipes at www.fbnr.com

Some of the products listed in this publication may be in limited distribution.

Recipe development on pages 3, 6, 22, 30, 36, 42, 76, 112, 122 and 148 by Bev Bennett.
Recipe development on pages 10, 14, 16, 18, 24, 46, 68, 72, 96 and 100 by Karen Levin.

Front cover photography and photography on pages 3, 7, 11, 15, 17, 19, 23, 25, 31, 37, 43, 47, 69, 73, 77, 97, 101, 113, 123 and 149 by Proffitt Photography, Chicago.
Photographer: Laurie Proffitt
Photographer's Assistant: Chad Evans
Food Stylist: Carol Smoler
Assistant Food Stylist: Sheila Grannen

Pictured on the front cover: Chicken with Pomegranate-Orange Sauce *(page 42)*.
Pictured on the back cover: Fan-Tailed Chinese Shrimp *(page 18)*.

ISBN-13: 978-1-4127-2954-3
ISBN-10: 1-4127-2954-8

Library of Congress Control Number: 2008923334

Manufactured in China.

8 7 6 5 4 3 2 1

Microwave Cooking: Microwave ovens vary in wattage. Use the cooking times as guidelines and check for doneness before adding more time.

Preparation/Cooking Times: Preparation times are based on the approximate amount of time required to assemble the recipe before cooking, baking, chilling or serving. These times include preparation steps such as measuring, chopping and mixing. The fact that some preparations and cooking can be done simultaneously is taken into account. Preparation of optional ingredients and serving suggestions is not included.

appetizers
& soups

crab rangoon with spicy dipping sauce

1 cup ketchup
¼ cup chili garlic sauce
4 teaspoons Chinese hot mustard
1 package (8 ounces) cream cheese, softened
1 can (6 ounces) lump crabmeat, well drained
⅓ cup minced green onions, green parts only
1 package (12 ounces) wonton wrappers
1 egg white, beaten
Vegetable oil for frying

1. For sauce, combine ketchup, chili garlic sauce and mustard in small bowl; set aside.

2. Beat cream cheese in medium bowl until light and fluffy. Stir in crabmeat and green onions.

3. Arrange wonton wrappers, 1 at a time, on clean work surface. Place 1 rounded teaspoon crab mixture in center. Brush inside edges of wonton wrapper with egg white. Fold wonton diagonally in half to form triangle (wonton wrappers are not quite square so they will not form perfect triangles); press edges firmly to seal.

4. Heat 2 inches oil in Dutch oven or deep skillet. Add wontons, a few at a time. Fry on one side 2 minutes or until golden; turn and fry 2 minutes or until second side is golden. Remove with slotted spoon and drain on paper towel-lined plate. Serve immediately with sauce for dipping. *Makes about 12 servings*

Variation: Crab Rangoon can be baked instead of fried, but the results will not be as crisp or as golden in color. Prepare as directed through Step 3, then arrange triangles 1 inch apart on parchment-lined baking sheets. Spray tops of triangles with nonstick cooking spray. Bake in preheated 375°F oven about 11 minutes or until lightly browned. Serve immediately.

appetizers
& soups

ginger plum spareribs

1 jar (10 ounces) damson plum preserves or apple jelly
⅓ cup KARO® Light or Dark Corn Syrup
⅓ cup soy sauce
¼ cup chopped green onions
2 cloves garlic, minced
2 teaspoons ground ginger
2 pounds pork spareribs, trimmed, cut into serving pieces

1. In small saucepan combine preserves, corn syrup, soy sauce, green onions, garlic and ginger. Stirring constantly, cook over medium heat until melted and smooth.

2. Pour into 11×7×2-inch baking dish. Add ribs, turning to coat. Cover; refrigerate several hours or overnight, turning once.

3. Remove ribs from marinade; place on rack in shallow baking pan.

4. Bake in 350°F oven about 1 hour or until tender, turning occasionally and basting with marinade. Do not baste during last 5 minutes of cooking. *Makes about 20 servings*

Ginger Plum Chicken Wings: Omit spareribs. Follow recipe for Ginger Plum Spareribs. Use 2½ pounds chicken wings, separated at the joints (tips discarded). Bake 45 minutes, basting with marinade during last 30 minutes. Do not baste during last 5 minutes of cooking.

Prep Time: 15 minutes, plus marinating
Bake Time: 1 hour

ginger plum spareribs

sweet-hot orange chicken drumettes

¼ cup plus 3 tablespoons orange juice, divided

4 tablespoons orange marmalade or apricot jam, divided

3 tablespoons hoisin sauce

1 teaspoon grated fresh ginger

10 chicken drumettes (about 1¼ pounds)

3 tablespoons chili garlic sauce

¼ teaspoon salt

¼ teaspoon red pepper flakes

⅛ teaspoon five-spice powder (optional)

⅛ teaspoon black pepper

   Sesame seeds (optional)

1. Preheat oven to 400°F. Line baking sheet with heavy-duty foil; generously spray foil with nonstick cooking spray.

2. Combine ¼ cup orange juice, 2 tablespoons orange marmalade, hoisin sauce and ginger in medium microwavable bowl. Microwave on HIGH 1 minute or until marmalade melts; stir until well blended.

3. Dip drumettes, 1 at a time, in orange juice mixture; place on prepared baking sheet. Bake 15 minutes; turn and bake 5 to 10 minutes or until drumettes are golden brown and cooked through.

4. Meanwhile, prepare sauce. Combine remaining 3 tablespoons orange juice, 2 tablespoons orange marmalade, chili garlic sauce, salt, red pepper flakes, five-spice powder, if desired, and black pepper in small microwavable bowl. Microwave on HIGH 1 minute or until marmalade melts; stir until well blended.

5. To serve, arrange drumettes on platter. Garnish with sesame seeds; serve with dipping sauce.

Makes about 5 servings

wonton soup

¼ **pound ground pork, chicken or turkey**
¼ **cup finely chopped water chestnuts**
2 **tablespoons soy sauce, divided**
1 **egg white, lightly beaten**
1 **teaspoon minced fresh ginger**
12 **wonton wrappers**
1 **can (46 ounces) chicken broth**
1½ **cups sliced spinach leaves**
1 **cup thinly sliced cooked pork (optional)**
½ **cup diagonally sliced green onions**
1 **tablespoon dark sesame oil**
Shredded carrot (optional)

1. For wonton filling, combine ground pork, water chestnuts, 1 tablespoon soy sauce, egg white and ginger in small bowl; mix well.

2. Place 1 wonton wrapper with point toward edge of counter. Mound 1 teaspoon filling near bottom point. Fold bottom point over filling, then roll wrapper over once. Moisten inside points with water. Bring side points together below filling, overlapping slightly; press together firmly to seal. Repeat with remaining wrappers and filling.* Keep finished wontons covered with plastic wrap while filling remaining wrappers.

3. Combine broth and remaining 1 tablespoon soy sauce in large saucepan; bring to a boil over high heat. Reduce heat to medium; add wontons. Simmer, uncovered, 4 minutes, or until filling is cooked through.

4. Stir in spinach, sliced pork, if desired, and green onions; remove from heat. Stir in sesame oil. Ladle into soup bowls. Garnish with carrot.   *Makes 2 servings*

*Wontons may be made ahead to this point; cover and refrigerate up to 8 hours or freeze up to 3 months. Proceed as directed above if using refrigerated wontons; increase simmering time to 6 minutes if using frozen wontons.

wonton soup

chinese crab cakes

1 pound fresh or canned pasteurized lump crabmeat*
1 cup panko bread crumbs, divided
2 eggs
2 green onions, finely chopped
1 tablespoon dark sesame oil
2 teaspoons grated fresh ginger
2 teaspoons Chinese hot mustard
2 tablespoons peanut or canola oil, divided
½ cup sweet and sour sauce

*Choose special grade crabmeat for this recipe. It is less expensive and already flaked but just as flavorful as backfin, lump or claw meat. Look for it in the refrigerated seafood section of the supermarket. Shelf-stable canned crabmeat can be substituted.

1. Combine crabmeat, ⅔ cup panko, eggs, green onions, sesame oil, ginger and mustard in large bowl; mix well.

2. Shape level ⅓ cupfuls of mixture into 8 patties about ½ inch thick. (At this point patties may be covered and chilled up to 2 hours.)

3. Heat 1 tablespoon peanut oil in large nonstick skillet over medium heat. Place remaining ⅓ cup panko in shallow dish. Dip each crab cake lightly in panko to coat. Add 4 crab cakes to skillet; cook 3 to 4 minutes per side or until golden brown and heated through. (Crab cakes will be soft, so turn them carefully.) Keep warm. Repeat with remaining 1 tablespoon oil and 4 crab cakes. Serve with sweet and sour sauce.

Makes 4 servings

shantung twin mushroom soup

1 package (1 ounce) dried shiitake mushrooms
2 teaspoons vegetable oil
1 large onion, coarsely chopped
2 cloves garlic, minced
2 cups sliced button mushrooms
2 cans (about 14 ounces each) reduced-sodium chicken broth
2 ounces cooked ham, cut into thin slivers
½ cup thinly sliced green onions
1 tablespoon dry sherry
1 tablespoon reduced-sodium soy sauce
1 tablespoon cornstarch

1. Place dried mushrooms in small bowl; cover with boiling water. Soak 20 minutes to soften. Drain; squeeze out excess water. Discard stems; slice caps.

2. Heat oil in large saucepan over medium heat. Add chopped onion and garlic; cook 1 minute. Add dried and button mushrooms; cook 4 minutes, stirring occasionally.

3. Add broth; bring to a boil over high heat. Reduce heat to medium; simmer, covered, 15 minutes.

4. Stir in ham and green onions; cook until heated through. Stir sherry and soy sauce into cornstarch in small bowl until smooth; stir into soup. Cook 2 minutes or until soup is thickened, stirring occasionally.

Makes 6 servings

shantung twin mushroom soup

szechwan chicken cucumber cups

1½ cups finely shredded or chopped cooked skinless rotisserie chicken
1 tablespoon rice vinegar
1 tablespoon soy sauce
1½ teaspoons dark sesame oil
1 teaspoon grated fresh ginger
⅛ teaspoon red pepper flakes
1 large seedless cucumber (about 1 pound)
¼ cup chopped fresh cilantro

1. Combine chicken, vinegar, soy sauce, sesame oil, ginger and red pepper flakes in medium bowl; mix well.

2. Trim off ends of cucumber. Use fork to score all sides of cucumber lengthwise (or peel cucumber lengthwise in alternating strips). Cut cucumber crosswise into 20 (½-inch) slices. Use melon baller or grapefruit spoon to scoop out indentation in one cut side of each slice to form cup.

3. Mound 1 tablespoon chicken mixture in indentation in each cup. Sprinkle with cilantro. Serve immediately or cover and chill up to 2 hours before serving. *Makes 10 servings*

egg drop soup

4 cups chicken broth
2 tablespoons soy sauce
1 tablespoon dry sherry
1 tablespoon water
1 tablespoon cornstarch
2 eggs, well beaten
2 green onions, thinly sliced diagonally
2 teaspoons dark sesame oil

1. Combine broth, soy sauce and sherry in large saucepan; bring to a boil over high heat. Reduce heat to low; simmer 2 minutes.

2. Stir water into cornstarch in small bowl until smooth. Stir mixture into soup; simmer 2 to 3 minutes or until slightly thickened.

3. Stirring constantly in one direction, slowly add beaten eggs to soup in thin stream. Stir in green onions. Remove from heat; stir in sesame oil. Serve immediately.

Makes 4 servings

fan-tailed chinese shrimp

     1 tablespoon seasoned rice vinegar
     1 tablespoon oyster sauce
     1 tablespoon soy sauce
     2 cloves garlic, minced
   ¼ teaspoon red pepper flakes
   18 large raw shrimp (about 1 pound), peeled and deveined (with tails on)
     1 tablespoon peanut or canola oil
   ¼ cup chopped fresh cilantro
       Plum sauce or sweet and sour sauce (optional)

1. For marinade, combine combine vinegar, oyster sauce, soy sauce, garlic and red pepper flakes in large bowl; mix well.

2. To butterfly shrimp, use small sharp knife to cut each shrimp down back (where vein was) three quarters of the way through shrimp. Open shrimp; place cut side down on work surface, pressing to flatten into butterfly shape. Add shrimp to bowl with marinade; toss to coat. Cover and refrigerate at least 30 minutes or up to 2 hours.

3. Heat oil in large nonstick skillet over medium heat. Remove shrimp from marinade; discard marinade. Cook shrimp (in batches if necessary) 3 to 4 minutes, turning once, until shrimp are pink and opaque. Transfer to serving platter; sprinkle with cilantro. Serve with plum sauce for dipping, if desired.   *Makes 6 servings*

chinatown stuffed mushrooms

24 large mushrooms (about 1 pound)
½ pound ground turkey
1 clove garlic, minced
¼ cup dry bread crumbs
¼ cup thinly sliced green onions
3 tablespoons reduced-sodium soy sauce, divided
1 egg white, lightly beaten
1 teaspoon minced fresh ginger
⅛ teaspoon red pepper flakes (optional)

1. Remove stems from mushrooms; finely chop enough stems to equal 1 cup. Cook turkey, chopped stems and garlic in medium skillet over medium-high heat until turkey is no longer pink, stirring to break up meat. Drain fat. Stir in bread crumbs, green onions, 2 tablespoons soy sauce, egg white, ginger and red pepper flakes, if desired; mix well.

2. Preheat broiler. Line broiler pan with foil; top with broiler rack. Spray broiler rack with nonstick cooking spray.

3. Brush mushroom caps lightly with remaining 1 tablespoon soy sauce; spoon about 2 teaspoons stuffing into each mushroom cap.* Place stuffed mushrooms on prepared broiler rack. Broil 4 to 5 inches from heat 5 to 6 minutes or until heated through. *Makes 12 servings*

*Mushrooms can be made ahead to this point; cover and refrigerate up to 24 hours. Add 1 to 2 minutes to broiling time for chilled mushrooms. Or, freeze filling in individual portions. To freeze, place portions on cookie sheet or shallow pan; place in freezer 30 minutes to firm slightly. Transfer to freezer food storage bag and freeze completely. Thaw in refrigerator before filling mushrooms as directed.

pork and noodle soup

1 package (1 ounce) dried shiitake mushrooms
4 ounces thin egg noodles
6 cups chicken broth
2 cloves garlic, minced
½ cup shredded carrot
4 ounces Canadian bacon, cut into short thin strips
1 tablespoon hoisin sauce
⅛ teaspoon black pepper
2 tablespoons minced fresh chives

1. Place mushrooms in heatproof bowl; add boiling water to cover. Soak 20 minutes to soften. Drain; squeeze out excess water. Discard stems; slice caps.

2. Meanwhile, cook egg noodles according to package directions just until tender. Drain and set aside.

3. Combine broth and garlic in large saucepan; bring to a boil over high heat. Reduce heat to low. Add mushrooms, carrot, Canadian bacon, hoisin sauce and pepper to saucepan; simmer 15 minutes. Add noodles; simmer until heated through. Sprinkle with chives just before serving. *Makes 6 servings*

hoisin-orange chicken wraps

¼ cup orange juice
¼ cup hoisin sauce
½ teaspoon grated orange peel
8 whole Boston lettuce leaves
2 cups shredded coleslaw mix
2 cups diced cooked chicken (about 8 ounces)
Black pepper (optional)

Combine orange juice, hoisin sauce and orange peel in small bowl. Arrange lettuce leaves on large serving platter. Place ¼ cup coleslaw mix, ¼ cup chicken and 1 tablespoon hoisin mixture on each leaf. Sprinkle with pepper, if desired. Fold lettuce over to create bundles. *Makes 4 servings*

pork and noodle soup

mini egg rolls

½ **pound ground pork**
3 **cloves garlic, minced**
1 **teaspoon minced fresh ginger**
¼ **teaspoon red pepper flakes**
6 **cups (12 ounces) shredded coleslaw mix**
¼ **cup reduced-sodium soy sauce**
1 **tablespoon cornstarch**
1 **tablespoon seasoned rice vinegar**
½ **cup chopped green onions**
28 **wonton wrappers**
   Peanut or canola oil for frying
   Sweet and sour sauce
   Chinese hot mustard (optional)

1. Combine pork, garlic, ginger and red pepper flakes in large nonstick skillet; cook and stir over medium heat about 4 minutes or until pork is no longer pink. Add coleslaw mix; cover and cook 2 minutes. Uncover and cook 2 minutes or until coleslaw mix is wilted but crisp-tender.

2. Stir soy sauce into cornstarch in small bowl until smooth. Stir into pork mixture with vinegar; cook 2 to 3 minutes or until sauce thickens. Remove from heat; stir in green onions.

3. To fill egg rolls, place one wonton wrapper on clean work surface with one point facing you. Spoon 1 level tablespoon pork mixture across and just below center of wrapper. Fold bottom point of wrapper up over filling; fold side points over filling, forming envelope shape. Moisten inside edges of top point with water and roll egg roll toward top point, pressing firmly to seal. Repeat with remaining wrappers and filling.

4. Heat about ¼ inch oil in large skillet over medium heat; fry egg rolls in small batches about 2 minutes per side or until golden brown. Drain on paper towels; serve warm with sweet and sour sauce and hot mustard, if desired, for dipping.

Makes 28 mini egg rolls

fried tofu with sesame dipping sauce

3 tablespoons soy sauce

2 tablespoons unseasoned rice wine vinegar

2 teaspoons sugar

1 teaspoon sesame seeds, toasted*

1 teaspoon dark sesame oil

⅛ teaspoon red pepper flakes

1 block (about 12 ounces) extra-firm tofu

2 tablespoons all-purpose flour

1 egg

¾ cup panko bread crumbs

4 tablespoons vegetable oil, divided

*To toast sesame seeds, spread seeds in small skillet. Shake skillet over medium-low heat about 3 minutes or until seeds begin to pop and turn golden.

1. For dipping sauce, combine soy sauce, vinegar, sugar, sesame seeds, sesame oil and red pepper flakes in small bowl. Set aside.

2. Drain tofu and press between paper towels to remove excess water. Cut crosswise into 4 slices; cut each slice diagonally into triangles. Place flour in shallow dish. Beat egg in shallow bowl. Place panko in another shallow bowl.

3. Coat each piece of tofu lightly with flour on all sides, then dip in egg, turning to coat. Drain and roll in panko to coat lightly.

4. Heat 2 tablespoons vegetable oil in large nonstick skillet over high heat. Reduce heat to medium; add tofu in single layer. Cook 1 to 2 minutes per side or until golden brown. Repeat with remaining tofu. Serve with dipping sauce. *Makes 4 servings*

fried tofu with sesame
dipping sauce

quick hot and sour chicken soup

2 cups water

2 cups chicken broth

1 package (about 10 ounces) refrigerated fully cooked chicken breast strips, cut into pieces

1 package (about 7 ounces) reduced-sodium chicken-flavored rice and vermicelli mix

1 jalapeño pepper,* minced

2 green onions, chopped

1 tablespoon soy sauce

1 tablespoon lime juice

1 tablespoon minced fresh cilantro (optional)

*Jalapeño peppers can sting and irritate the skin, so wear rubber gloves when handling peppers and do not touch your eyes.

1. Combine water, broth, chicken, rice mix, jalapeño pepper, green onions and soy sauce in large saucepan; bring to a boil over high heat. Reduce heat to low; cover and simmer 20 minutes or until rice is tender, stirring occasionally.

2. Stir in lime juice; sprinkle with cilantro, if desired. *Makes 4 servings*

tip | Recipes often call for just a small amount of cilantro and leave you with almost an entire bunch. To keep cilantro fresh longer, store it in a glass of water, stem ends down, covered loosely with a plastic bag. It will keep in the refrigerator for up to one week.

baked pork buns

1 tablespoon vegetable oil
2 cups coarsely chopped bok choy
1 small onion or large shallot, thinly sliced
1 container (18 ounces) refrigerated barbecue shredded pork
 All-purpose flour
2 containers (about 10 ounces each) refrigerated buttermilk biscuits (10 biscuits total)

1. Preheat oven to 350°F. Grease large baking sheet.

2. Heat oil in large skillet over medium-high heat. Add bok choy and onion; cook and stir 8 to 10 minutes or until vegetables are tender. Remove from heat; stir in barbecue pork.

3. Lightly dust clean work surface with flour. Remove biscuits from containers and separate into individual biscuits. Working with 1 at a time, split biscuit in half crosswise to create two thin biscuits. Roll each biscuit half into 5-inch circle. Spoon heaping tablespoon pork mixture onto one side of circle. Fold dough over filling to form half circle; press edges to seal. Arrange buns on prepared baking sheet. Repeat with remaining biscuits and filling.

4. Bake 12 to 15 minutes or until golden brown. Serve warm. *Makes 20 buns*

soy-glazed chicken wings

2 tablespoons dry sherry

2 tablespoons soy sauce

1 tablespoon sugar

1 tablespoon cornstarch

3 teaspoons minced garlic, divided

1 teaspoon red pepper flakes

12 chicken wings (about 2½ pounds), tips removed and cut into halves

2 tablespoons vegetable oil

3 green onions, cut into 1-inch pieces

¼ cup chicken broth

1 teaspoon sesame oil

1 tablespoon sesame seeds, toasted*

*To toast sesame seeds, spread seeds in small skillet. Shake skillet over medium-low heat about 3 minutes or until seeds begin to pop and turn golden.

1. For marinade, combine sherry, soy sauce, sugar, cornstarch, 2 teaspoons minced garlic and red pepper flakes in large bowl; mix well. Stir in chicken wings; cover and marinate overnight in refrigerator, turning once or twice.

2. Drain chicken wings, reserving marinade. Heat wok or large skillet over high heat 1 minute. Add vegetable oil; heat 30 seconds. Add half of wings; cook 10 to 15 minutes or until wings are brown on all sides, turning occasionally. Remove with slotted spoon to bowl. Reheat oil in wok 30 seconds and repeat with remaining wings. Reduce heat to medium. Discard any remaining oil.

3. Add remaining 1 teaspoon garlic and green onions to wok; cook and stir 30 seconds. Add chicken wings and broth to wok; cover and cook 5 minutes or until wings are tender, stirring occasionally to prevent wings from sticking to bottom of wok.

4. Add reserved marinade; bring to a boil. Cook and stir 2 minutes or until wings are glazed with marinade. Add sesame oil; mix well. Transfer wings to serving platter; sprinkle with sesame seeds. Serve immediately.

Makes 2 dozen appetizers

appetizers & soups

shrimp toast

12 large raw shrimp, peeled and deveined (with tails on)
1 egg
2 tablespoons plus 1½ teaspoons cornstarch
¼ teaspoon salt
   Dash black pepper
3 slices white sandwich bread, each cut into 4 triangles
1 hard-cooked egg yolk, cut into ½-inch pieces
1 slice (1 ounce) cooked ham, cut into ½-inch pieces
1 green onion, finely chopped
   Vegetable oil for frying
   Sliced green onions (optional)

1. Cut deep slit down back of each shrimp; press gently with fingers to flatten.

2. Beat egg, cornstarch, salt and pepper in large bowl until blended. Add shrimp; toss to coat well.

3. Drain each shrimp and press, cut side down, into each piece of bread. Brush small amount of leftover egg mixture onto each shrimp.

4. Place 1 piece each of egg yolk and ham and scant ¼ teaspoon chopped green onion on top of each shrimp.

5. Heat about 1 inch oil in wok or large skillet over medium-high heat to 375°F. Add three or four bread pieces at a time; cook 1 to 2 minutes, then spoon hot oil over shrimp until cooked through and toast is golden brown. Drain on paper towels. Garnish with sliced green onions. *Makes 12 servings*

sizzling chicken

cashew chicken

  1 **pound boneless skinless chicken breasts or thighs**
  2 **teaspoons minced fresh ginger**
  1 **tablespoon peanut or vegetable oil**
  1 **medium red bell pepper, cut into short, thin strips**
  ⅓ **cup teriyaki sauce**
  ⅓ **cup roasted or dry roasted cashews**
     Hot cooked rice (optional)
     Coarsely chopped fresh cilantro (optional)

1. Cut chicken into ½-inch slices; cut each slice into 1½-inch strips. Toss chicken with ginger in small bowl.

2. Heat oil in wok or large skillet over medium-high heat. Add chicken mixture; stir-fry 2 minutes. Add bell pepper; stir-fry 4 minutes or until chicken is cooked through.

3. Add teriyaki sauce; stir-fry 1 minute or until sauce is heated through. Stir in cashews. Serve over rice, if desired. Garnish with cilantro.

Makes 4 servings

sizzling
chicken

lemon chicken

1 egg yolk
2 teaspoons soy sauce
1½ cups panko bread crumbs
⅛ teaspoon salt
⅛ teaspoon black pepper
1 pound chicken tenders or 1 pound boneless skinless chicken breasts,
    cut into long 1-inch-thick strips
1 cup chicken broth
1 tablespoon cornstarch
1 teaspoon vegetable oil
1 clove garlic, minced
    Grated peel of 1 small lemon
1 teaspoon sugar
1½ to 2½ teaspoons lemon juice
1 head broccoli, trimmed and cut into long, thin strips

1. Preheat oven to 400°F. Line baking sheet with parchment paper. Combine egg yolk and soy sauce in shallow bowl. Combine panko, salt and pepper on plate. Dip chicken strips in egg mixture, then coat with panko mixture. Arrange chicken on baking sheet in single layer (strips should not touch). Spray chicken with nonstick cooking spray.

2. Bake 10 minutes; turn and bake 10 to 13 minutes or until chicken is golden brown and cooked through.

3. Meanwhile, stir broth into cornstarch in small bowl until smooth. Heat oil in small saucepan over low heat. Add garlic; cook and stir 1 minute or until softened. Stir in lemon peel. Increase heat to medium. Stir cornstarch mixture; add to saucepan with sugar. Cook and stir 2 minutes or until thickened. Stir in 1½ teaspoons lemon juice; taste and add additional lemon juice, if desired.

4. Steam broccoli strips 5 minutes or until tender; drain well. Drizzle lemon sauce over chicken and broccoli.

Makes 4 servings

Tip: To add a touch of spice to the chicken, stir ⅛ teaspoon ground red pepper into the panko mixture.

ginger plum chicken

2 tablespoons oil
1 tablespoon thinly sliced fresh ginger
8 ounces chicken (boneless breast or thigh), cut into 1 inch pieces
3 tablespoons LEE KUM KEE® Premium Brand or Panda Brand or Choy Sun Oyster Sauce
½ red bell pepper, cut into 1-inch pieces
½ green bell pepper, cut into 1-inch pieces
1 carrot, cut into 1-inch strips
3 tablespoons LEE KUM KEE® Plum Sauce
1 green onion, chopped
  Hot cooked noodles

1. Heat oil in wok or skillet until hot. Add ginger; stir-fry 30 seconds. Add chicken and LEE KUM KEE Oyster Sauce; stir-fry until chicken is almost done.

2. Add bell peppers and carrot; stir-fry 1 to 2 minutes. Add LEE KUM KEE Plum Sauce and green onion; stir-fry until chicken is cooked through. Serve over noodles.   *Makes 2 servings*

Prep Time: 20 minutes
Cook Time: 10 to 12 minutes

tip | When purchasing fresh ginger, select roots with smooth, unwrinkled skin. To use, peel the tough skin away with a paring knife or vegetable peeler before slicing or mincing as the recipe directs. Peel only what is needed for the recipe, then tightly wrap the remaining ginger and store it in the refrigerator for up to three weeks.

ginger plum chicken

chinese chicken salad

    4 cups chopped bok choy
    3 cups diced cooked chicken breast
    1 cup shredded carrots
    2 tablespoons minced fresh chives or green onions
    2 tablespoons chili garlic sauce
 1½ tablespoons peanut or canola oil
    1 tablespoon balsamic vinegar
    1 tablespoon soy sauce
    1 teaspoon minced fresh ginger

1. Place bok choy, chicken, carrots and chives in large bowl.

2. Combine chili garlic sauce, oil, vinegar, soy sauce and ginger in small bowl; mix well. Pour over chicken mixture; toss gently. *Makes 4 servings*

simple stir-fry

     1 tablespoon vegetable oil
    12 boneless, skinless chicken breast tenderloins, cut into 1-inch pieces
     1 bag (1 pound) frozen stir-fry vegetable mix
     2 tablespoons soy sauce
     2 tablespoons honey
     2 (2-cup) bags UNCLE BEN'S® Boil-in-Bag Rice

1. Heat oil in large skillet or wok. Add chicken; cook over medium-high heat 6 to 8 minutes or until lightly browned. Add vegetables, soy sauce and honey. Cover and cook 5 to 8 minutes or until chicken is no longer pink in center and vegetables are crisp-tender.

2. Meanwhile, cook rice according to package directions. Serve stir-fry over rice. *Makes 4 servings*

chinese chicken salad

chicken with pomegranate-orange sauce

2 tablespoons soy sauce, divided

3 teaspoons cornstarch, divided

1 pound boneless skinless chicken breasts, cut into 1-inch cubes

½ cup pomegranate juice

1 to 2 tablespoons chili garlic sauce

1 teaspoon grated orange peel

1 teaspoon grated fresh ginger

1 tablespoon vegetable or peanut oil

2 stalks celery, cut diagonally into ¼-inch slices

1 small red bell pepper, cut into 1-inch-long strips

2 oranges, peeled and sectioned

3 green onions, sliced

2 cups hot cooked rice

1. Stir 1 tablespoon soy sauce into 1 teaspoon cornstarch in medium bowl until smooth. Add chicken; toss to coat. Cover; let stand 10 minutes.

2. Meanwhile, combine pomegranate juice, chili garlic sauce, remaining 1 tablespoon soy sauce, 2 teaspoons cornstarch, orange peel and ginger in small bowl. Stir until smooth; set aside.

3. Heat oil in wok or large nonskillet over medium-high heat. Add chicken; stir-fry 2 minutes. Add celery and bell pepper; stir-fry 3 minutes or until chicken is cooked through. Stir pomegranate juice mixture; add to wok. Bring to a boil over high heat; reduce heat to medium and simmer 1 minute. Gently stir in orange sections; cook until heated through. Sprinkle with green onions; serve with rice. *Makes 4 servings*

chicken with pomegranate-orange
sauce

sesame chicken

1 pound boneless skinless chicken breasts or thighs
⅓ cup teriyaki sauce
2 teaspoons cornstarch
1 tablespoon peanut or vegetable oil
2 cloves garlic, minced
2 green onions, cut into ½-inch slices
1 tablespoon sesame seeds, toasted*
1 teaspoon dark sesame oil

*To toast sesame seeds, spread seeds in small skillet. Shake skillet over medium-low heat 3 minutes or until seeds begin to pop and turn golden.

1. Cut chicken into 1-inch pieces; toss with teriyaki sauce in medium bowl. Marinate at room temperature 15 minutes or cover and refrigerate up to 2 hours.

2. Drain chicken, reserving marinade. Stir reserved marinade into cornstarch in small bowl until smooth; set aside.

3. Heat wok or large skillet over medium-high heat. Add peanut oil; heat 30 seconds. Add chicken and garlic; stir-fry 3 minutes or until chicken is cooked through. Stir cornstarch mixture; add to wok. Cook and stir 1 minute or until sauce boils and thickens. Stir in green onions, sesame seeds and sesame oil.

Makes 4 servings

sesame chicken

drunken roast chicken

  1 chicken (3 to 3½ pounds), quartered
  ¼ cup soy sauce
  ¼ cup dry sherry, divided
  4 cloves garlic, minced
  1 tablespoon minced fresh ginger
  ½ teaspoon red pepper flakes
  ½ cup plum sauce
  2 teaspoons Chinese hot mustard

1. Place chicken quarters in large resealable food storage bag. Combine soy sauce, 3 tablespoons sherry, garlic, ginger and red pepper flakes in small bowl; pour over chicken. Seal bag; turn to coat. Marinate chicken in refrigerator at least 30 minutes or up to 4 hours.

2. Meanwhile, combine plum sauce, mustard and remaining 1 tablespoon sherry in small bowl until well blended; set aside.

3. Preheat oven to 375°F. Line large baking sheet or jelly-roll pan with foil. Remove chicken from bag, reserving marinade. Place chicken on prepared baking sheet.

4. Bake 25 minutes. Brush reserved marinade over chicken; discard any remaining marinade. *Increase oven temperature to 450°F.* Bake 20 minutes or until internal temperature of thigh meat reaches 165°F. Serve chicken with plum sauce mixture.

Makes 4 servings

pineapple basil chicken supreme

1 can (8 ounces) pineapple chunks in unsweetened juice

2 teaspoons cornstarch

2 tablespoons peanut oil

1 pound boneless skinless chicken breasts, cut into ¾-inch pieces

2 to 4 serrano peppers,* cut into thin strips (optional)

2 cloves garlic, minced

2 green onions, cut into 1-inch pieces

¾ cup roasted unsalted cashews

¼ cup chopped fresh basil

1 tablespoon fish sauce**

1 tablespoon soy sauce

Hot cooked rice (optional)

*Serrano peppers can sting and irritate the skin, so wear rubber gloves when handling peppers and do not touch your eyes.

**Fish sauce is available at most large supermarkets and Asian markets.

1. Drain pineapple, reserving juice. Stir reserved juice into cornstarch in small bowl until smooth; set aside.

2. Heat wok or large skillet over high heat 1 minute. Drizzle oil into wok; heat 30 seconds. Add chicken, peppers, if desired, and garlic; stir-fry 3 minutes or until chicken is cooked through. Add green onions; stir-fry 1 minute.

3. Stir cornstarch mixture; add to wok. Cook and stir 1 minute or until thickened. Add pineapple, cashews, basil, fish sauce and soy sauce; cook and stir 1 minute or until heated through. Serve over rice, if desired.

Makes 4 servings

curry chicken stir-fry

healthy
chicken

½ cup reduced-sodium chicken broth

2 teaspoons cornstarch

2 teaspoons reduced-sodium soy sauce

1½ teaspoons curry powder

⅛ teaspoon red pepper flakes

4 teaspoons peanut or vegetable oil, divided

3 green onions, sliced

2 cloves garlic, minced

2 cups broccoli florets

⅔ cup sliced carrots

6 ounces boneless skinless chicken breasts, cut into bite-size pieces

Hot cooked rice

1. Stir broth, cornstarch, soy sauce, curry powder and red pepper flakes in small bowl until smooth; set aside.

2. Heat 2 teaspoons oil in nonstick wok or large skillet over medium-high heat. Add green onions and garlic; stir-fry 1 minute. Remove from wok.

3. Add broccoli and carrots to wok; stir-fry 2 to 3 minutes or until crisp-tender. Remove from wok.

4. Add remaining 2 teaspoons oil to hot wok. Add chicken; stir-fry 2 to 3 minutes or until cooked through. Stir cornstarch mixture; add to wok. Cook and stir until sauce comes to a boil and thickens slightly. Return all vegetables to wok; cook and stir until heated through. Serve over rice. *Makes 2 servings*

curry chicken stir-fry

chicken with lychees

¼ cup plus 1 teaspoon cornstarch, divided

1 pound boneless skinless chicken breasts, cut into bite-size pieces

½ cup water, divided

½ cup tomato sauce

1 teaspoon sugar

1 teaspoon chicken bouillon

3 tablespoons vegetable oil

6 green onions, cut into 1-inch pieces

1 red bell pepper, cut into 1-inch pieces

1 can (11 ounces) whole peeled lychees, drained

Cooked cellophane noodles (optional)

1. Place ¼ cup cornstarch in large resealable food storage bag; add chicken. Seal bag; shake until chicken is well coated.

2. Stir ¼ cup water into remaining 1 teaspoon cornstarch in small bowl until smooth; set aside. Combine tomato sauce, remaining ¼ cup water, sugar and chicken bouillon in medium bowl; set aside.

3. Heat oil in wok or large skillet over high heat. Add chicken; stir-fry 3 to 5 minutes or until lightly browned. Add green onions and bell pepper; stir-fry 1 minute.

4. Add tomato sauce mixture and lychees to wok. Reduce heat to low; cover and simmer 5 minutes or until chicken is cooked through.

5. Stir cornstarch mixture; add to wok. Cook and stir until sauce boils and thickens. Serve over cellophane noodles, if desired.

Makes 4 servings

chicken with lychees

kung po chicken

1 pound boneless skinless chicken breasts or thighs
2 cloves garlic, minced
1 teaspoon hot chili oil
¼ cup reduced-sodium soy sauce
2 teaspoons cornstarch
1 tablespoon peanut or vegetable oil
⅓ cup roasted peanuts
2 green onions, cut into short thin strips
   Lettuce leaves
   Plum sauce

1. Cut chicken into 1-inch pieces. Toss chicken with garlic and chili oil in medium bowl. Stir soy sauce into cornstarch in small bowl until smooth; set aside.

2. Heat wok or large skillet over medium-high heat. Add peanut oil; heat 30 seconds. Add chicken mixture; stir-fry 3 minutes or until chicken is cooked through.

3. Stir cornstarch mixture; add to wok with peanuts and green onions. Cook and stir 1 minute or until sauce boils and thickens.

4. To serve, spread lettuce leaves lightly with plum sauce. Top with chicken mixture.　　*Makes 4 servings*

kung po chicken

chicken stir-fry with cabbage pancake

2 cups shredded coleslaw mix
2 eggs, beaten
1 teaspoon reduced-sodium soy sauce
½ teaspoon white pepper
1 pound asparagus, trimmed, cut into 1-inch pieces
1 package (8 ounces) sliced mushrooms
1 pound chicken tenders, cut into 1-inch pieces
1 teaspoon minced fresh ginger, divided
1 teaspoon minced garlic, divided
1 teaspoon dark sesame oil, divided
½ cup water
1 tablespoon cornstarch

1. For pancake, combine coleslaw mix, eggs, soy sauce and white pepper in large bowl until well blended. Spray large nonstick skillet with nonstick cooking spray; heat over medium-high heat. Pour coleslaw mixure into skillet; cover and cook 4 minutes or until set and browned. Turn pancake and cook, uncovered, about 2 minutes. Keep warm.

2. For stir-fry, spray large nonstick skillet with cooking spray; heat over medium-high heat. Add asparagus; stir-fry 1 to 2 minutes. Add mushrooms; stir-fry 2 minutes. Add chicken, ½ teaspoon ginger, ½ teaspoon garlic and ½ teaspoon sesame oil; stir-fry 3 minutes or until chicken is cooked through.

3. Combine water, cornstarch, remaining ½ teaspoon ginger, garlic and sesame oil in small bowl until smooth. Add to skillet; cook and stir 1 to 2 minutes or until sauce thickens slightly.

4. Cut pancake into 4 wedges. Spoon stir-fry over each wedge.

Makes 4 servings

**chicken stir-fry with
cabbage pancake**

moo goo gai pan

1 package (1 ounce) dried shiitake mushrooms
¼ cup reduced-sodium soy sauce
2 tablespoons rice vinegar
3 cloves garlic, minced
1 pound boneless skinless chicken breasts
½ cup chicken broth
1 tablespoon cornstarch
2 tablespoons peanut or vegetable oil, divided
1 can (about 7 ounces) straw mushrooms, rinsed and drained
3 green onions, cut into 1-inch pieces
  Hot cooked Chinese egg noodles or rice (optional)

1. Place dried mushrooms in small bowl; cover with boiling water. Soak 20 minutes to soften. Drain; squeeze out excess water. Discard stems; slice caps.

2. Combine soy sauce, vinegar and garlic in medium bowl. Cut chicken crosswise into ½-inch strips. Add to soy sauce mixture; toss to coat. Marinate at room temperature 20 minutes. Stir broth into cornstarch in small bowl until smooth; set aside.

3. Heat wok or large skillet over medium-high heat. Add 1 tablespoon oil; heat 30 seconds. Drain chicken, reserving marinade. Add chicken to wok; stir-fry 3 minutes or until cooked through. Remove and set aside. Heat remaining 1 tablespoon oil in wok. Add dried mushrooms, straw mushrooms and green onions; stir-fry 1 minute.

4. Stir cornstarch mixture; add to wok with reserved marinade. Bring to a boil; boil 1 minute or until sauce thickens. Return chicken along with any accumulated juices to wok; cook and stir until heated through. Serve over noodles, if desired.

Makes 4 servings

moo goo gai pan

easy make-at-home chinese chicken

3 tablespoons frozen orange juice concentrate, thawed
2 tablespoons water
2 tablespoons reduced-sodium soy sauce
¾ teaspoon cornstarch
¼ teaspoon garlic powder
2 carrots, cut into ¼-inch slices
1 package (12 ounces) frozen broccoli and cauliflower florets, thawed
1 tablespoon peanut or vegetable oil
¾ pound boneless skinless chicken breasts, cut into bite-size pieces
   Hot cooked rice

1. For sauce, combine orange juice concentrate, water, soy sauce, cornstarch and garlic powder in small bowl until smooth; set aside.

2. Spray nonstick wok or large skillet with nonstick cooking spray; heat over high heat. Add carrots; stir-fry 1 minute. Add broccoli and cauliflower; stir-fry 2 to 3 minutes or until vegetables are crisp-tender. Remove vegetables from wok; set aside.

3. Add oil to wok; heat over medium-high heat. Add chicken; stir-fry 2 to 3 minutes or until cooked through. Push chicken up side of wok. Stir sauce; add to wok. Bring to a boil. Return vegetables to wok; cook and stir until heated through. Serve over rice. *Makes 4 servings*

Tip: To cut carrots decoratively, use a citrus stripper or grapefruit spoon to cut 4 or 5 grooves into whole carrots, cutting lengthwise from stem end to tip. Then cut carrots crosswise into slices.

chicken chow mein

1 pound boneless skinless chicken breasts, cut into thin strips

2 cloves garlic, minced

2 teaspoons peanut oil, divided

2 tablespoons dry sherry

2 tablespoons reduced-sodium soy sauce

2 cups (about 7 ounces) fresh snow peas, cut into halves *or* 1 package (7 ounces) frozen snow peas, thawed

3 green onions, cut diagonally into 1-inch pieces

1½ cups Chinese egg noodles or vermicelli, cooked and drained (4 ounces uncooked)

1 teaspoon dark sesame oil (optional)

1. Toss chicken and garlic in medium bowl.

2. Heat 1 teaspoon peanut oil in wok or large nonstick skillet over medium-high heat. Add chicken and garlic; stir-fry 3 minutes or until chicken is cooked through. Transfer to medium bowl; toss with sherry and soy sauce.

3. Heat remaining 1 teaspoon peanut oil in wok. Add snow peas; stir-fry 2 minutes for fresh or 1 minute for thawed frozen snow peas. Add green onions; stir-fry 30 seconds. Add chicken mixture; stir-fry 1 minute.

4. Add noodles to wok; stir-fry 2 minutes or until heated through. Stir in sesame oil, if desired.

Makes 4 servings

tip | Peanut oil has a faint peanut flavor and a high smoke point, which makes it a good choice for frying and stir-frying. Dark sesame oil has a strong flavor and is typically used in small amounts to add flavor to a dish. It is not used for frying, but can be used for stir-frying when its flavor is essential to the dish.

orange chicken stir-fry

½ cup orange juice

2 tablespoons sesame oil, divided

2 tablespoons soy sauce

1 tablespoon dry sherry

2 teaspoons freshly grated fresh ginger

1 teaspoon freshly grated orange peel

1 clove garlic, minced

1½ pounds boneless skinless chicken breasts, cut into strips

3 cups mixed fresh vegetables, such as green bell pepper, red bell pepper, snow peas, carrots, green onions, mushrooms and/or onions

1 tablespoon cornstarch

½ cup unsalted cashew bits or halves

3 cups hot cooked rice

Combine orange juice, 1 tablespoon oil, soy sauce, sherry, ginger, orange peel and garlic in large glass bowl. Add chicken; marinate in refrigerator 1 hour. Drain chicken, reserving marinade. Heat remaining 1 tablespoon oil in large skillet or wok over medium-high heat. Add chicken; stir-fry 3 minutes or until chicken is light brown. Add vegetables; stir-fry 3 to 5 minutes or until vegetables are crisp-tender. Combine cornstarch and marinade; add to skillet and stir until sauce boils and thickens. Stir in cashews; cook 1 minute more. Serve over hot rice.

Makes 6 servings

Favorite recipe from **USA Rice**

beef
& pork

cashew beef

2 tablespoons cooking oil

8 ounces beef (flank steak, skirt steak, top sirloin or fillet mignon), cut into strips ¼ inch thick

3 tablespoons LEE KUM KEE® Premium Brand, Panda Brand or Choy Sun Oyster Sauce

¼ cup *each* red and green bell pepper strips (1-inch strips)

2 stalks celery, cut into ½-inch slices

½ cup carrot slices (½-inch slices)

¼ cup small button mushrooms halves

2 tablespoons LEE KUM KEE® Soy Sauce

1 green onion, chopped

2 tablespoons cashews, toasted*

1 tablespoon LEE KUM KEE® Chili Garlic Sauce or Sriracha Chili Sauce

*Cashews can be toasted in wok or skillet prior to cooking.

1. Heat wok or skillet over high heat until hot. Add oil, beef and LEE KUM KEE Oyster Sauce; cook until beef is half done.

2. Add bell peppers, celery, carrots, mushrooms and LEE KUM KEE Soy Sauce; stir-fry until vegetables are crisp-tender and beef is cooked through. Stir in green onion and cashews. Add Chili Garlic Sauce or Sriracha Chili Sauce for spiciness or use as dipping sauce.

Makes 2 servings

beef
& pork

sweet and sour pork

1 tablespoon soy sauce
2 cloves garlic, minced
1 lean boneless pork loin or tenderloin roast* (about 1 pound)
1 can (8 ounces) pineapple chunks in juice, undrained
2 tablespoons peanut or vegetable oil, divided
2 medium carrots, diagonally cut into thin slices
1 large green bell pepper, cut into 1-inch pieces
⅓ cup stir-fry sauce
1 tablespoon white wine or white vinegar
   Hot cooked rice (optional)

*Or, substitute 1 pound boneless skinless chicken breasts or thighs.

1. Combine soy sauce and garlic in medium bowl. Cut pork across the grain into 1-inch pieces; toss with soy sauce mixture. Drain pineapple, reserving 2 tablespoons juice.

2. Heat wok or large skillet over medium-high heat. Add 1 tablespoon oil; heat 30 seconds. Add pork mixture; stir-fry 4 to 5 minutes or until pork is no longer pink. Remove pork to medium bowl.

3. Heat remaining 1 tablespoon oil in wok. Add carrots and bell pepper; stir-fry 4 to 5 minutes or until vegetables are crisp-tender. Add pineapple; stir-fry until heated through.

4. Add stir-fry sauce, reserved pineapple juice and vinegar to wok; cook and stir 30 seconds or until sauce comes to a boil. Return pork along with any accumulated juices to wok; cook and stir until heated through. Serve over rice, if desired. *Makes 4 servings*

red cooked pork roast

1 tablespoon peanut or canola oil
3 to 3½ pounds boneless pork shoulder roast (pork butt)
½ cup chicken broth
¼ cup soy sauce
4 cloves garlic, minced
3 whole star anise
1 tablespoon water
1 tablespoon cornstarch
4 drops red food coloring
   Hot cooked Chinese noodles or rice

1. Heat oil in Dutch oven or large deep ovenproof skillet with lid over medium heat. Add pork; cook until browned, 6 to 7 minutes per side.

2. Meanwhile, preheat oven to 325°F. Combine broth, soy sauce, garlic and star anise in small bowl; pour over pork in Dutch oven. Cover and bake 3 hours or until pork is very tender when pierced with fork. Transfer to cutting board; tent with foil.

3. Discard star anise; skim off and discard fat from pan juices. Stir water into cornstarch in small bowl until smooth. Place Dutch oven with pan juices over medium heat; stir in cornstarch mixture. Bring to a boil, stirring constantly. Simmer 2 to 3 minutes or until sauce thickens. Stir in food coloring.

4. Cut meat into chunks (or shred with 2 forks); return to Dutch oven to toss with sauce and heat through. Serve with noodles. *Makes 6 to 8 servings*

tip | Star anise is a dark brown, star-shaped pod that comes from a small Chinese evergreen tree. This spice is used whole to flavor broths, cooking liquids and liqueurs; it is also ground and used as an ingredient in Chinese five-spice powder. Both star anise and five-spice powder can be found in Asian markets and the spice aisles of many supermarkets.

one pan pork fu yung

1 cup reduced-sodium chicken broth
1 tablespoon cornstarch
½ teaspoon dark sesame oil, divided
2 teaspoons canola oil
½ pound boneless pork tenderloin, chopped
5 green onions, thinly sliced, divided
1 cup sliced mushrooms
¼ teaspoon salt
¼ teaspoon white pepper
1 cup bean sprouts
2 eggs
2 egg whites

1. Combine broth, cornstarch and ¼ teaspoon sesame oil in small saucepan. Cook and stir over medium heat 5 to 6 minutes or until sauce thickens.

2. Heat canola oil in large nonstick skillet over medium-high heat. Add pork; stir-fry about 4 minutes or until no longer pink.

3. Reserve 2 tablespoons green onion. Add mushrooms, remaining green onions, ¼ teaspoon sesame oil, salt and pepper to skillet; stir-fry 4 to 5 minutes or until mushrooms are lightly browned. Add sprouts; stir-fry 1 minute. Flatten mixture in skillet with spatula.

4. Beat eggs and egg whites in medium bowl; pour over pork mixture in skillet. Reduce heat to low. Cover and cook about 3 minutes or until eggs are set.

5. Cut into 4 wedges. Top each wedge with sauce and sprinkle with reserved green onion.

Makes 4 servings

Serving Suggestion: Serve with a lettuce wrap salad. Separate Boston lettuce leaves and arrange on a platter with grated carrot, radish slices, seedless cucumber rounds, red bell pepper strips and bean sprouts. Serve with a dipping sauce made by whisking together 1 cup reduced-sodium chicken broth, 1 tablespoon rice vinegar, ¼ teaspoon sesame oil, ¼ teaspoon minced fresh ginger and ¼ teaspoon minced garlic.

spicy chinese pepper steak

1 (1-pound) boneless beef top sirloin steak, cut into thin strips
1 tablespoon cornstarch
3 cloves garlic, minced
½ teaspoon red pepper flakes
2 tablespoons peanut or canola oil, divided
1 green bell pepper, cut into thin strips
1 red bell pepper, cut into thin strips
¼ cup oyster sauce
2 tablespoons soy sauce
3 tablespoons chopped fresh cilantro or green onions

1. Combine beef, cornstarch, garlic and red pepper flakes in medium bowl; toss to coat.

2. Heat 1 tablespoon oil in wok or large skillet over medium-high heat. Add bell peppers; stir-fry 3 minutes. Transfer peppers to medium bowl. Add remaining 1 tablespoon oil and beef mixture to wok; stir-fry 4 to 5 minutes or until beef is barely pink in center.

3. Add oyster sauce and soy sauce to wok; stir-fry 1 minute. Return peppers to wok; stir-fry 1 to 2 minutes or until sauce thickens. Sprinkle with cilantro just before serving.   *Makes 4 servings*

savory pork stir-fry

  1 pound lean boneless pork loin
  1 tablespoon vinegar
  1 tablespoon soy sauce
  1 teaspoon sesame oil
  1 clove garlic, minced
  ½ teaspoon ground ginger
  1 teaspoon vegetable oil
  1 (10-ounce) package frozen stir-fry vegetables, unthawed
  1 tablespoon chicken broth or water
    Hot cooked rice (optional)
  1 tablespoon toasted sesame seeds (optional)

Slice pork across grain into ⅛-inch strips. Marinate in vinegar, soy sauce, sesame oil, garlic and ginger for 10 minutes. Heat vegetable oil in nonstick pan until hot. Add pork mixture and stir-fry for 3 to 5 minutes or until pork is no longer pink. Add vegetables and chicken broth. Stir mixture, cover and steam until vegetables are crisp-tender. Serve over hot cooked rice and sprinkle with toasted sesame seeds, if desired.

Makes 4 servings

Prep Time: 20 minutes

Favorite recipe from **National Pork Board**

sesame beef with pineapple-plum sauce

3 tablespoons soy sauce, divided

3½ teaspoons cornstarch, divided

1 pound beef flank steak, cut into thin strips across the grain

2 teaspoons grated fresh ginger

2 cloves garlic, minced

⅛ teaspoon red pepper flakes

1 package (12 ounces) fresh refrigerated pineapple spears or chunks*

1 tablespoon sesame seeds

1 tablespoon vegetable oil

¼ cup chicken broth

¼ cup slivered red bell pepper

2 tablespoons plum sauce

¼ cup minced green onions, green parts only, plus additional for garnish

*Fresh pineapple spears packed in plastic containers can be found in supermarket produce departments. If unavailable, use 1½ cups canned pineapple chunks packed in unsweetened juice.

1. Stir 2 tablespoons soy sauce into 1½ teaspoons cornstarch in medium bowl until smooth. Add beef, ginger, garlic and red pepper flakes; toss to coat. Let stand 30 minutes. Drain pineapple, reserving juice. Stir 2 tablespoons pineapple juice into remaining 2 teaspoons cornstarch in small bowl until smooth; set aside. Cut pineapple spears into chunks.

2. Toast sesame seeds in large heavy skillet over medium-low heat 3 minutes or until golden. Immediately remove from skillet; set aside.

3. Heat oil in same skillet over medium-high heat. Add beef, being careful not to crowd skillet (cook in two batches, if necessary). Cook 2 minutes per side or until beef is browned and barely pink in center.

4. Stir pineapple juice-cornstarch mixture; add to skillet. Add broth, bell pepper, plum sauce, remaining 1 tablespoon soy sauce and green onions to skillet; cook and stir 1 minute or until sauce thickens. Stir in pineapple chunks; cook and stir until heated through. Sprinkle sesame seeds; garnish with additional green onions.

Makes 4 servings

sesame beef with pineapple-plum sauce

barbecued pork

¼ cup soy sauce
2 tablespoons dry red wine
1 green onion, sliced
1 tablespoon brown sugar
1 tablespoon honey
2 teaspoons red food coloring (optional)
1 clove garlic, minced
½ teaspoon ground cinnamon
2 whole pork tenderloins (about 12 ounces each), trimmed
Hot cooked rice (optional)

1. Combine soy sauce, wine, green onion, sugar, honey, food coloring, if desired, garlic and cinnamon in large bowl. Add pork; turn to coat completely. Cover and refrigerate 1 hour or overnight, turning pork occasionally.

2. Preheat oven to 350°F. Drain pork, reserving marinade. Place pork on wire rack in baking pan. Bake 30 to 45 minutes or until thermometer inserted into center of pork registers 160°F, turning and basting frequently with reserved marinade during first 30 minutes of cooking. Discard any remaining marinade.

3. Remove pork from oven; let rest 5 minutes. Cut into diagonal slices. Serve with rice, if desired.

Makes about 4 servings

orange beef

1 pound boneless beef top sirloin or tenderloin steaks
2 cloves garlic, minced
1 teaspoon grated orange peel
2 tablespoons orange juice
2 tablespoons soy sauce
1 tablespoon dry sherry
1 tablespoon cornstarch
1 tablespoon peanut or vegetable oil
2 cups hot cooked rice (optional)
   Orange peel strips or orange slices (optional)

1. Cut beef in half lengthwise, then cut crosswise into thin slices. Toss with garlic and grated orange peel in medium bowl.

2. Stir orange juice, soy sauce and sherry into cornstarch in small bowl until smooth; set aside.

3. Heat wok or large skillet over medium-high heat; add oil. Stir-fry beef in batches 2 to 3 minutes or until barely pink in center. Stir cornstarch mixture; add to wok. Cook and stir 30 seconds or until sauce boils and thickens. Serve over rice, if desired; garnish with orange peel strips. *Makes 4 servings*

exotic pork & vegetables

¼ cup water

2 teaspoons cornstarch

4 tablespoons peanut oil, divided

6 whole dried hot red chili peppers

4 cloves garlic, sliced

1 pork tenderloin (about ¾ pound), thinly sliced

1 large carrot, cut into ¼-inch-thick slices*

2 ounces fresh oyster, shiitake or button mushrooms,** cut into halves

1 baby eggplant, thinly sliced

5 ounces snow peas, ends trimmed

3 tablespoons packed brown sugar

2 tablespoons fish sauce

1 tablespoon dark sesame oil

Hot cooked rice

*To make scalloped edges on carrot, use citrus stripper or grapefruit spoon to cut groove into carrot, cutting lengthwise from stem end to tip. Continue to cut grooves around carrot about ¼ inch apart. Then cut carrot crosswise into ¼-inch-thick slices.

**Or, substitute ½ ounce dried shiitake mushrooms, soaked according to package directions.

1. Stir water into cornstarch in small bowl until smooth; set aside.

2. Heat wok or large skillet over high heat 1 minute. Add 2 tablespoons peanut oil into wok; heat 30 seconds. Add peppers and garlic; stir-fry 1 minute. Add pork; stir-fry 3 to 4 minutes or until no longer pink. Remove pork mixture to bowl.

3. Add remaining 2 tablespoons peanut oil to wok. Add carrot, mushrooms and eggplant; stir-fry 2 minutes. Add snow peas and pork mixture; stir-fry 1 minute.

4. Stir cornstarch mixture; add to wok. Cook 1 minute or until sauce is thickened. Stir in brown sugar, fish sauce and sesame oil; cook and stir until heated through. Serve with rice. *Makes 4 servings*

exotic pork & vegetables

mongolian hot pot

2 ounces cellophane noodles (bean threads)*
½ pound boneless beef top sirloin or tenderloin steaks
   Dipping Sauce (recipe follows)
1 can (46 ounces) chicken broth
½ pound pork tenderloin, cut into ⅛-inch slices
½ pound medium raw shrimp, peeled and deveined
½ pound sea scallops, cut lengthwise into halves
½ pound small mushrooms
1 pound spinach leaves

*Cellophane noodles, also called bean threads or glass noodles, are clear, thin noodles sold in tangled bunches.

1. Place cellophane noodles in medium bowl; cover with boiling water. Soak 10 minutes or until soft and pliable. Drain well. Cut noodles into 1- to 2-inch lengths; set aside.

2. Cut beef lengthwise in half, then cut crosswise into ⅛-inch slices. Prepare Dipping Sauce.

3. Heat broth in electric skillet to a simmer (or bring half of broth to simmer in fondue pot, keeping remaining broth hot for replacement).

4. Arrange beef, pork, shrimp, scallops and mushrooms on large platter. To serve, select food from platter and cook in simmering broth until cooked through, using chopsticks or long-handled fork. Serve with Dipping Sauce.

5. After all food is cooked, stir spinach into broth and heat until wilted. (Cook spinach in two batches if using fondue pot.) Place cellophane noodles in individual soup bowls. Ladle broth mixture into bowls. Season with remaining Dipping Sauce, if desired.   *Makes 4 to 6 servings*

Dipping Sauce: Combine ½ cup reduced-sodium soy sauce, ¼ cup dry sherry and 1 tablespoon dark sesame oil in small bowl. Transfer to individual dipping bowls.

beef & pork

chinese pork & vegetable stir-fry

2 tablespoons BERTOLLI® Olive Oil, divided

1 pound pork tenderloin or boneless beef sirloin, cut into ¼-inch slices

6 cups assorted fresh vegetables*

1 can (8 ounces) sliced water chestnuts, drained

1 envelope LIPTON® RECIPE SECRETS® Onion Soup Mix

¾ cup water

½ cup orange juice

1 tablespoon soy sauce

¼ teaspoon garlic powder

*Use any combination of the following: broccoli florets; thinly sliced red or green bell peppers; snow peas or thinly sliced carrots.

1. In 12-inch skillet, heat 1 tablespoon olive oil over medium-high heat; brown pork. Remove and set aside.

2. In same skillet, heat remaining 1 tablespoon olive oil and cook assorted fresh vegetables, stirring occasionally, 5 minutes. Stir in water chestnuts, soup mix blended with water, orange juice, soy sauce and garlic powder. Bring to a boil over high heat. Reduce heat to low and simmer uncovered, 3 minutes. Return pork to skillet and cook 1 minute or until heated through. *Makes about 4 servings*

sesame-garlic flank steak

1 beef flank steak (about 1¼ pounds)
2 tablespoons soy sauce
2 tablespoons hoisin sauce
1 tablespoon dark sesame oil
2 cloves garlic, minced

1. Score steak lightly with sharp knife in diamond pattern on both sides; place in large resealable food storage bag. Combine soy sauce, hoisin sauce, sesame oil and garlic in small bowl; pour over steak. Seal bag; turn to coat. Marinate in refrigerator at least 2 hours or up to 24 hours, turning once.

2. Prepare grill for direct cooking.

3. Drain steak, reserving marinade. Place on grid over medium heat. Grill, covered, 13 to 18 minutes for medium-rare to medium or until desired doneness, turning and brushing with marinade halfway through cooking time. Discard any remaining marinade.

4. Transfer steak to cutting board; carve across the grain into thin slices.

Makes 4 servings

sesame-garlic flank steak and
stir-fried spinach with garlic
(page 140)

better-than-take-out fried rice

3 tablespoons reduced-sodium soy sauce

1 tablespoon rice vinegar

$\frac{1}{8}$ teaspoon red pepper flakes

1 medium red bell pepper

1 tablespoon peanut or vegetable oil

6 green onions, cut into 1-inch pieces

1 tablespoon grated fresh ginger

1$\frac{1}{2}$ teaspoons minced garlic

8 ounces boneless pork loin or tenderloin, cut into 1-inch pieces

2 cups shredded coleslaw mix

1 package (8$\frac{1}{2}$ ounces) cooked whole grain brown rice

1. Combine soy sauce, vinegar and red pepper flakes in small bowl; mix well. Set aside.

2. Remove and discard stem and seeds from bell pepper. Cut pepper into decorative shapes with 1$\frac{1}{4}$- to 1$\frac{1}{2}$-inch cookie cutters, or cut into 1-inch pieces.

3. Heat oil in wok or large nonstick stillet over medium-high heat. Add bell pepper, green onions, ginger and garlic; stir-fry 1 minute. Add pork; stir-fry 2 to 3 minutes or until pork is no longer pink. Stir in coleslaw mix, rice and soy sauce mixture; cook and stir 1 minute or until heated through. *Makes 4 servings*

Prep Time: 15 minutes

five-spice beef stir-fry

1 boneless beef top sirloin steak (about 1 pound)
2 tablespoons reduced-sodium soy sauce
2 tablespoons plus 1½ teaspoons cornstarch, divided
3 tablespoons walnut or vegetable oil, divided
4 medium carrots, cut into matchstick-size pieces (about 2 cups)
1 red bell pepper, cut into 1-inch pieces
1 yellow bell pepper, cut into 1-inch pieces
1 cup chopped onion
¼ to ½ teaspoon red pepper flakes
1½ cups water
1 tablespoon plus 1½ teaspoons packed dark brown sugar
2 teaspoons beef bouillon
1 teaspoon Chinese five-spice powder*
3 cups hot cooked rice
½ cup honey-roasted peanuts

*Chinese five-spice powder is a blend of cinnamon, cloves, fennel seed, anise and Szechuan peppercorns. It is available in most supermarkets and at Asian grocery stores.

1. Cut beef in half lengthwise, then cut crosswise into thin strips. Place beef in shallow glass dish. Stir soy sauce into 2 tablespoons cornstarch in small bowl until smooth. Pour soy sauce mixture over beef; stir to coat.

2. Meanwhile, heat 1 tablespoon oil in wok or large nonstick skillet over high heat 1 minute. Add carrots; stir-fry 3 to 4 minutes or until edges begin to brown. Remove carrots from wok. Reduce heat to medium-high. Add 1 tablespoon oil, bell peppers, onion and red pepper flakes to wok; stir-fry 4 minutes or until onion is translucent. Remove bell pepper mixture from wok; set aside separately from carrots.

3. Add remaining 1 tablespoon oil to wok. Add half of beef; stir-fry 2 minutes or until beef is barely pink in center. Remove to large bowl. Repeat with remaining beef.

4. Meanwhile, stir water, brown sugar, beef bouillon, five-spice powder and remaining 1½ teaspoons cornstarch in small bowl until well blended. Add bouillon mixture and bell pepper mixture to wok; bring to a boil. Cook and stir 2 to 3 minutes or until sauce is slightly thickened.

5. Toss rice with carrots; place on serving platter. Spoon beef mixture over rice; sprinkle with peanuts.

Makes 4 servings

five-spice beef stir-fry

szechuan pork stir-fry over spinach

2 teaspoons dark sesame oil, divided
¾ cup matchstick-size carrot strips
½ pound lean pork tenderloin, cut into thin strips
3 cloves garlic, minced
2 teaspoons minced fresh ginger
¼ to ½ teaspoon red pepper flakes
1 tablespoon dry sherry
1 tablespoon reduced-sodium soy sauce
2 teaspoons cornstarch
8 ounces baby spinach leaves
2 teaspoons sesame seeds, toasted*

*To toast sesame seeds, spread in small skillet. Shake skillet over medium-low heat about 3 minutes or until seeds begin to pop and turn golden.

1. Heat 1 teaspoon oil in large nonstick skillet over medium-high heat. Add carrots; stir-fry 3 minutes. Add pork, garlic, ginger and red pepper flakes; stir-fry 3 minutes or until pork is no longer pink.

2. Stir sherry and soy sauce into cornstarch in small bowl until smooth; add to skillet. Cook and stir 1 minute or until sauce thickens.

3. Heat remaining 1 teaspoon oil in medium saucepan over medium-high heat. Add spinach; cover and cook 1 minute or until spinach is barely wilted. Transfer spinach to 2 serving plates; spoon pork mixture over spinach. Sprinkle with sesame seeds.   *Makes 2 servings*

szechwan pork stir-fry over spinach

chinese peppercorn beef

2 teaspoons whole black and/or pink peppercorns

2 teaspoons coriander seeds

1 tablespoon peanut or canola oil

1 boneless beef top sirloin steak, about 1¼ inches thick (1¼ to 1½ pounds)

2 teaspoons dark sesame oil

½ cup thinly sliced shallots or sweet onion

½ cup chicken broth

2 tablespoons soy sauce

1 tablespoon dry sherry

1 tablespoon water

1 teaspoon cornstarch

2 tablespoons thinly sliced green onion or chopped fresh cilantro

1. Place peppercorns and coriander seeds in small resealable food storage bag; seal bag. Coarsely crush spices using meat mallet or bottom of heavy saucepan. Brush peanut oil over both sides of steak; sprinkle with peppercorn mixture, pressing in lightly.

2. Heat large heavy skillet over medium-high heat until hot. Add steak; cook 4 minutes or until seared on bottom. Reduce heat to medium; turn steak and continue cooking 3 to 4 minutes for medium-rare or until desired doneness. Transfer steak to carving board; tent with foil and let stand while preparing sauce.

3. Add sesame oil to same skillet; heat over medium heat. Add shallots; cook and stir 3 minutes. Add broth, soy sauce and sherry; simmer 2 minutes.

4. Stir water into cornstarch in small bowl until smooth. Add to skillet; cook and stir 3 to 4 minutes or until sauce thickens. Carve steak crosswise into thin slices. Spoon sauce over steak; sprinkle with green onion.

Makes 4 servings

black bean and chili garlic beef

  2 tablespoons cooking oil

  8 ounces beef (top sirloin, skirt steak, flank steak or fillet mignon), cut into strips ¼ inch thick

  2 tablespoons LEE KUM KEE® Black Bean Garlic Sauce

  ¼ cup sliced celery

  ¼ cup small button mushrooms, cut into halves

  ¼ cup sliced carrots

  1 tablespoon LEE KUM KEE® Chili Garlic Sauce

  1 green onion, chopped

  1 tablespoon LEE KUM KEE® Pure Sesame Oil

Heat wok or skillet over high heat until hot. Add cooking oil, beef and LEE KUM KEE Black Bean Garlic Sauce; cook until beef is half done. Add celery, mushrooms, carrots and LEE KUM KEE Chili Garlic Sauce; stir-fry until beef is done. Sprinkle with green onion and LEE KUM KEE Pure Sesame Oil.   *Makes 2 servings*

citrus spiced pork lo mein

  6 ounces linguine

  4 teaspoons HERB-OX® chicken flavored bouillon, divided

  8 ounces pork tenderloin, halved lengthwise and cut into ¼-inch strips

  2 teaspoons vegetable oil

  2 cups sliced bok choy

  ¾ cup water

  ¼ cup orange juice

  2 tablespoons soy sauce

  2 teaspoons sesame oil

  ½ teaspoon red pepper flakes

  1 (11-ounce) can mandarin oranges, drained

Cook noodles according to package directions, adding 2 teaspoons of bouillon to cooking liquid. Meanwhile, in wok or large skillet, stir-fry pork in hot vegetable oil for 3 minutes. Add bok choy and cook for additional 3 to 4 minutes or until pork is cooked through and bok choy is crisp-tender. Add water, orange juice, remaining bouillon, soy sauce, sesame oil and red pepper flakes to pork mixture. Bring to a boil. Stir in prepared noodles and stir for 1 minute. Remove mixture from heat and gently stir in oranges.   *Makes 4 servings*

sensational seafood

beijing fillet of sole

2 tablespoons reduced-sodium soy sauce
2 teaspoons dark sesame oil
4 sole fillets (about 6 ounces each)
1¼ cups shredded cabbage or coleslaw mix
½ cup crushed chow mein noodles
1 egg white, lightly beaten
2 teaspoons sesame seeds

1. Preheat oven to 350°F. Line shallow baking pan with foil. Combine soy
sauce and oil in small bowl. Place sole in shallow dish. Lightly brush both sides of sole with soy sauce mixture.

2. Combine cabbage, noodles, egg white and remaining soy sauce mixture in medium bowl. Spoon evenly in
center of each fillet. Roll up fillets. Place seam side down in prepared pan.

3. Sprinkle rolls with sesame seeds. Bake 25 to 30 minutes or until fish begins to flake when tested with fork.

Makes 4 servings

sensational
seafood

sweet & sour shrimp on garlic spinach

    1 tablespoon peanut or canola oil
1½ pounds large raw shrimp, peeled and deveined
    1 tablespoon minced fresh ginger
    ⅓ cup sweet and sour sauce
    3 tablespoons soy sauce, divided
    2 tablespoons seasoned rice vinegar
    2 teaspoons Chinese hot mustard
    2 teaspoons dark sesame oil
    3 cloves garlic, thinly sliced
    2 packages (9 ounces each) baby spinach leaves

1. Heat peanut oil in large skillet over medium heat. Add shrimp and ginger; stir-fry 2 minutes. Add sweet and sour sauce, 1 tablespoon soy sauce, vinegar and mustard; stir-fry 3 to 4 minutes or until shrimp are pink and opaque and sauce has thickened. Remove from heat; cover to keep warm.

2. Meanwhile, heat sesame oil in large saucepan or Dutch oven over medium heat. Add garlic; cook and stir 1 minute. Add half of spinach; cook, turning frequently with tongs, about 1 minute until spinach begins to wilt. Add remaining spinach and remaining 2 tablespoons soy sauce; cook and stir 1 minute or just until spinach is barely wilted.

3. Transfer spinach to four plates; top with shrimp mixture.   *Makes 4 servings*

tip | Using tongs is the easiest way to turn large amounts of spinach when cooking. Spinach wilts quickly and should be turned constantly to avoid overcooking.

pan-cooked bok choy salmon

1 pound bok choy or napa cabbage, chopped
1 cup broccoli slaw mix
2 tablespoons peanut oil, divided
2 salmon fillets (4 to 6 ounces each)
¼ teaspoon salt
½ teaspoon black pepper
1 teaspoon sesame seeds

1. Combine bok choy and broccoli slaw mix in colander; rinse and drain well.

2. Heat 1 tablespoon oil in large nonstick skillet over medium heat. Sprinkle salmon with salt and pepper. Add salmon to skillet; cook about 3 minutes per side. Remove salmon from skillet.

3. Add remaining 1 tablespoon oil and sesame seeds to skillet; stir to toast sesame seeds. Add bok choy mixture; cook and stir 3 to 4 minutes.

4. Return salmon to skillet. Reduce heat to low; cover and cook about 4 minutes or until salmon begins to flake when tested with fork. Season with additional salt and pepper, if desired. *Makes 2 servings*

pan-cooked bok choy salmon

stir-fried crab

8 ounces firm tofu, drained
1 tablespoon soy sauce
¼ cup chicken broth
3 tablespoons oyster sauce
2 teaspoons cornstarch
1 tablespoon peanut or vegetable oil
2 cups snow peas, cut into halves
8 ounces thawed frozen cooked crabmeat or imitation crabmeat, broken into ½-inch pieces (about 2 cups)
   Sesame Noodle Cake (recipe follows)
2 tablespoons chopped fresh cilantro or thinly sliced green onion

1. Press tofu lightly between paper towels; cut into ½-inch squares or triangles. Place in shallow dish; drizzle with soy sauce. Stir broth and oyster sauce into cornstarch in small bowl until smooth; set aside.

2. Heat oil in wok or large skillet over medium-high heat. Add snow peas; stir-fry 2 minutes or until crisp-tender. Add crabmeat; stir-fry 1 minute. Stir cornstarch mixture; add to wok. Cook and stir 30 seconds or until sauce boils and thickens.

3. Stir in tofu mixture; cook and stir until heated through. Serve over Sesame Noodle Cake; sprinkle with cilantro. *Makes 4 servings*

sesame noodle cake

4 ounces uncooked thin Chinese egg noodles or vermicelli
1 tablespoon soy sauce
1 tablespoon peanut or vegetable oil
½ teaspoon dark sesame oil

1. Cook noodles according to package directions; drain. Toss noodles with soy sauce.

2. Heat peanut oil in large nonstick skillet over medium heat. Add noodle mixture; pat into even layer with spatula. Cook 6 minutes or until bottom is browned. Invert onto plate, then slide back into skillet, browned side up. Cook 4 minutes or until bottom is browned. Drizzle with sesame oil. Transfer to serving platter and cut into quarters. *Makes 4 servings*

noodles with baby shrimp

1 package (about 4 ounces) cellophane noodles
3 green onions
1 tablespoon vegetable oil
1 package (16 ounces) frozen mixed vegetables (such as cauliflower, broccoli and carrots)
1 cup vegetable broth
8 ounces frozen baby shrimp
1 tablespoon soy sauce
2 teaspoons dark sesame oil
¼ teaspoon black pepper

1. Place noodles in large bowl. Cover with boiling water; let stand 10 to 15 minutes or just until softened. Drain noodles; cut into 5- or 6-inch pieces. Cut green onions into 1-inch pieces.

2. Heat wok over high heat about 1 minute. Drizzle vegetable oil into wok; heat 30 seconds. Add green onions; stir-fry 1 minute. Add mixed vegetables; stir-fry 2 minutes. Add broth; bring to a boil. Reduce heat to low; cover and cook 5 minutes or until vegetables are crisp-tender.

3. Add shrimp to wok; cook just until thawed. Stir in noodles, soy sauce, sesame oil and pepper; stir-fry until heated through.

Makes 4 to 6 servings

seafood

steamed fish fillets with black bean sauce

1½ pounds white-fleshed fish fillets (Lake Superior whitefish, halibut, rainbow trout or catfish)
1 tablespoon vegetable oil
2 green onions, chopped
2 tablespoons chopped fresh ginger
2 tablespoons black bean sauce (see tip)
Hot cooked rice (optional)
Green onion slivers (optional)

1. Fill large saucepan about one-third full with water. Place bamboo steamer basket over saucepan. Or, fill wok fitted with rack about one-third full with water. Cover and bring water to a boil. Place fillets in single layer on platter that fits into steamer or wok.

2. Heat oil in small skillet over medium-high heat. Add green onions, ginger and black bean sauce; cook and stir about 30 seconds or just until fragrant. Immediately pour contents of skillet over fillets. Place platter in steamer; cover and steam 10 to 15 minutes or until fish begins to flake when tested with fork.

3. Serve fillets and sauce over rice, if desired. Garnish with green onion slivers. *Makes 4 servings*

tip | Jarred black bean sauce is sold in the Asian food section of most large supermarkets. It is made of fermented black soybeans, soy sauce, garlic, sherry, sesame oil and ginger. Black soybeans have a pungent odor and a unique, pronounced flavor. Do not substitute regular black beans.

sensational
seafood

steamed fish fillets with
black bean sauce

easy seafood stir-fry

1 package (1 ounce) dried shiitake mushrooms*
½ cup reduced-sodium chicken broth
2 tablespoons dry sherry
1 tablespoon reduced-sodium soy sauce
4½ teaspoons cornstarch
2 teaspoons vegetable oil, divided
½ pound bay scallops or halved sea scallops
¼ pound medium raw shrimp, peeled and deveined
2 cloves garlic, minced
2 cups snow peas, cut diagonally into halves
2 cups hot cooked rice
¼ cup thinly sliced green onions

*Or substitute 1½ cups sliced fresh mushrooms. Omit step 1.

1. Place mushrooms in small bowl; cover with boiling water. Soak 20 minutes to soften. Drain; squeeze out excess water. Discard stems; slice caps.

2. Stir broth, sherry and soy sauce into cornstarch in another small bowl until smooth; set aside.

3. Heat 1 teaspoon oil in wok or large nonstick skillet over medium heat. Add scallops, shrimp and garlic; stir-fry 3 minutes or until seafood is opaque. Remove from wok.

4. Add remaining 1 teaspoon oil to wok. Add mushrooms and snow peas; stir-fry 3 minutes or until snow peas are crisp-tender.

5. Stir cornstarch mixture; add to wok. Cook and stir 2 minutes or until sauce boils and thickens. Return seafood and any accumulated juices to wok; cook and stir until heated through. Serve with rice; sprinkle with green onions.

Makes 4 servings

red snapper with orange-plum sauce

    1 pound red snapper fillets
    2 tablespoons reduced-sodium soy sauce
    ½ cup all-purpose flour
    ¼ teaspoon salt
    ⅛ teaspoon pepper
    2 to 3 tablespoons plus 1 teaspoon vegetable oil, divided
    ½ cup orange juice
    1 teaspoon cornstarch
    1 clove garlic, minced
    1 jalapeño pepper,* seeded and minced
    ½ cup plum sauce
    2 tablespoons mirin (rice wine)
    1 tablespoon chili garlic sauce
    1 tablespoon minced green onion, green part only (optional)

*Jalapeño peppers can sting and irritate the skin, so wear rubber gloves when handling peppers and do not touch your eyes.

1. Combine snapper fillets and soy sauce in shallow bowl; turn to coat all sides. Let stand 30 minutes.

2. Combine flour, salt and pepper on plate. Remove fish from soy sauce; coat with flour mixture.

3. Heat 2 tablespoons oil in large nonstick skillet. Place fish in skillet; shake skillet so fish doesn't stick. (Fillets should not touch in skillet; it may be necessary to cook fish in two batches.) Cook over medium-high heat 4 to 5 minutes per side. Remove fish from skillet and keep warm. If cooking fish in two batches, add 1 tablespoon oil to skillet and heat before adding remaining fish.

4. While fish is cooking, stir orange juice into cornstarch in small bowl until smooth. Heat remaining 1 teaspoon oil in small saucepan over medium-high heat. Add garlic and jalapeño pepper; cook and stir 1 minute. Add cornstarch mixture, plum sauce, mirin and chili garlic sauce; cook and stir 1 minute or until slightly thickened.

5. Arrange fish on plates and top with sauce; garnish with green onion.   *Makes 4 servings*

red snapper with
orange-plum sauce

shrimp in mock lobster sauce

½ cup reduced-sodium beef or chicken broth
¼ cup oyster sauce
1 tablespoon cornstarch
1 egg
1 egg white
1 tablespoon peanut or canola oil
¾ pound medium or large raw shrimp, peeled and deveined
2 cloves garlic, minced
3 green onions, cut into ½-inch pieces
2 cups hot cooked Chinese egg noodles

1. Stir broth and oyster sauce into cornstarch in small bowl until smooth; set aside. Beat egg and egg white in separate small bowl.

2. Heat wok over medium-high heat 1 minute. Drizzle oil into wok; heat 30 seconds. Add shrimp and garlic; stir-fry 3 to 5 minutes or until shrimp are pink and opaque.

3. Stir cornstarch mixture; add to wok. Add green onions; cook and stir 1 minute or until sauce boils and thickens.

4. Stir eggs into wok; cook and stir 1 minute or just until eggs are set. Serve over noodles.

Makes 4 servings

Note: Oyster sauce is a rich-tasting, dark brown sauce made from oysters, soy sauce and, often, MSG. Check the label to see if the sauce you're purchasing contains real oyster extract or just oyster flavoring. After opening, store oyster sauce in the refrigerator.

lemon sesame scallops

1 tablespoon sesame seeds
8 ounces uncooked whole wheat spaghetti
2 tablespoons sesame oil, divided
1 pound sea scallops
¼ cup chicken broth or clam juice
3 tablespoons lemon juice
2 tablespoons oyster sauce
1 tablespoon soy sauce
1 tablespoon cornstarch
½ teaspoon grated lemon peel
1 tablespoon vegetable oil
2 carrots, cut into matchstick-size strips
1 yellow bell pepper, cut into thin strips
4 slices peeled fresh ginger
1 clove garlic, minced
6 ounces fresh snow peas, trimmed or 1 (6-ounce) package frozen snow peas, thawed
2 green onions, thinly sliced

1. Heat small skillet over medium-low heat. Add sesame seeds; cook and stir 3 minutes or until golden.

2. Cook spaghetti according to package directions; drain. Place in large bowl; toss with 1 tablespoon sesame oil. Cover to keep warm.

3. Rinse scallops and pat dry with paper towels. Blend broth, lemon juice, oyster sauce, soy sauce, cornstarch and lemon peel in small bowl until smooth; set aside. Heat remaining 1 tablespoon sesame oil and vegetable oil in wok or large skillet over medium heat. Add carrots and bell pepper; stir-fry 4 to 5 minutes or until crisp-tender. Transfer to large bowl.

4. Increase heat to medium-high. Add ginger and garlic to wok; stir-fry 1 minute. Add scallops; stir-fry 1 minute. Add snow peas and green onions; stir-fry 3 minutes or until scallops are opaque. Remove and discard ginger. Transfer scallop mixture to bowl with vegetables, leaving any liquid in wok.

5. Stir cornstarch mixture; add to wok. Cook and stir 5 minutes or until thickened. Return scallop mixture to wok; cook 1 minute. Serve immediately over warm spaghetti; sprinkle with sesame seeds.

Makes 4 servings

shrimp & vegetable stir-fry

        1 tablespoon vegetable or peanut oil
      ½ medium red or yellow bell pepper, cut into strips
      ½ medium onion, cut into wedges
      10 snow peas, trimmed and cut diagonally into halves
        1 clove garlic, minced
        6 ounces medium cooked shrimp
        2 tablespoons stir-fry sauce
        1 cup hot cooked rice

1. Heat oil in wok or large nonstick skillet over medium-high heat. Add bell pepper, onion and snow peas; stir-fry 4 minutes. Add garlic; stir-fry 1 minute or until vegetables are crisp-tender.

2. Add shrimp and stir-fry sauce to wok; stir-fry 1 to 2 minutes or until heated through. Serve over rice.

Makes 2 servings

broiled hunan fish fillets

        3 tablespoons reduced-sodium soy sauce
        1 tablespoon finely chopped green onion
        2 teaspoons dark sesame oil
        1 clove garlic, minced
        1 teaspoon minced fresh ginger
      ¼ teaspoon red pepper flakes
        1 pound red snapper, scrod or cod fillets

1. Combine soy sauce, green onion, oil, garlic, ginger and red pepper flakes in small bowl.

2. Spray rack of broiler pan with nonstick cooking spray. Place fish on rack; brush with soy sauce mixture.

3. Broil 4 to 5 inches from heat 10 minutes or until fish begins to flake when tested with fork.

Makes 4 servings

shrimp & vegetable stir-fry

grilled chinese salmon

3 tablespoons soy sauce
2 tablespoons dry sherry
2 cloves garlic, minced
1 pound salmon fillets or steaks
2 tablespoons finely chopped fresh cilantro

1. Combine soy sauce, sherry and garlic in shallow dish. Add salmon; turn to coat. Cover; marinate in refrigerator at least 30 minutes or up to 2 hours.

2. Prepare grill for direct cooking. Remove salmon from dish, reserving marinade. Arrange fillets, skin side down, on oiled grid over hot coals or oiled rack of broiler pan. Grill or broil 10 minutes or until fish begins to flake when tested with fork. Baste with reserved marinade after 5 minutes of cooking; discard any remaining marinade. Sprinkle with cilantro. *Makes 4 servings*

tip | It is always helpful to grease your grill grid with oil or cooking spray before use to prevent food from sticking and to assist in cleanup, but it's especially crucial when grilling fish since fish is so delicate and can fall apart easily when moved. If you use cooking spray, spray the grid when cold—spraying a hot grill over the fire could cause a flare-up.

grilled chinese salmon

chili ginger shrimp

1 tablespoon plus 2 teaspoons soy sauce, divided

1 tablespoon plus 1½ teaspoons vegetable oil, divided

2 teaspoons grated fresh ginger

2 teaspoons lemon juice, divided

1 pound jumbo raw shrimp, peeled and deveined

2 tablespoons chili garlic sauce

⅛ teaspoon black pepper

Hot cooked rice (optional)

2 tablespoons minced fresh cilantro

1. Combine 1 tablespoon soy sauce, 1½ teaspoons oil, ginger and 1 teaspoon lemon juice in large bowl. Add shrimp; toss to coat. Cover and refrigerate 1 hour. Combine chili garlic sauce, remaining 2 teaspoons soy sauce, 1 teaspoon lemon juice and pepper in small bowl; set aside.

2. Heat remaining 1 tablespoon oil in wok or large deep skillet over medium-high heat. Drain shrimp, reserving marinade. Add shrimp to wok; stir-fry 6 minutes or until shrimp are pink and opaque.

3. Add reserved marinade and chili garlic sauce mixture to wok; cook and stir 1 minute or until sauce boils and thickens slightly. Serve over rice, if desired; sprinkle with cilantro before serving.   *Makes 4 servings*

chili ginger shrimp

stir-fried catfish with cucumber rice

    1 seedless cucumber
1¼ cups water
  ½ cup uncooked rice
  4 green onions, thinly sliced
  ½ teaspoon white pepper
  1 tablespoon peanut or vegetable oil
  1 pound catfish fillets, cut into 1-inch chunks
  1 teaspoon minced fresh ginger
  1 clove garlic, minced
  ¼ teaspoon dark sesame oil
12 ounces snow peas
  1 red bell pepper, diced
  ¼ cup white wine or water
  1 tablespoon cornstarch

1. Grate cucumber on medium side of grater into colander set over bowl; drain.

2. Combine water, rice, grated cucumber, green onions and white pepper in medium saucepan; bring to a boil over medium heat. Cover; reduce heat to low. Cook about 20 minutes or until rice is tender and liquid is absorbed.

3. Heat peanut oil in wok or large nonstick skillet over high heat. Add catfish, ginger, garlic and sesame oil; stir-fry 4 to 5 minutes or until catfish is just cooked. Add snow peas and bell pepper; cover and cook 4 minutes.

4. Stir wine into cornstarch in small bowl until smooth. Pour over catfish mixture; cook and stir about 2 minutes or until sauce thickens. Serve over rice mixture.   *Makes 4 servings*

stir-fried catfish with cucumber rice

seafood with basil and chilies

8 ounces cleaned squid (body tubes, tentacles or a combination)
8 ounces sea scallops
8 to 12 ounces medium raw shrimp, peeled
¼ cup water
2 tablespoons oyster sauce
1 teaspoon cornstarch
1 tablespoon vegetable oil
3 to 4 jalapeño peppers,* seeded and thinly sliced
6 cloves garlic, minced
½ cup roasted peanuts, salted or unsalted
2 green onions, thinly sliced
½ cup slivered fresh basil leaves
   Hot cooked rice

*Jalapeño peppers can sting and irritate the skin, so wear rubber gloves when handling peppers and do not touch your eyes.

1. Rinse squid; cut body tubes crosswise into ⅓-inch rings. Rinse and drain scallops. Slice large scallops crosswise into halves. Stir water and oyster sauce into cornstarch in small bowl until smooth; set aside.

2. Fill medium saucepan half full with water. Bring to a boil over high heat. Add shrimp; reduce heat to medium. Cook 2 to 3 minutes or until shrimp are pink and opaque. Remove to colander with slotted spoon. Return water to a boil. Add squid; cook rings over medium heat 1 minute. Cook tentacles 4 minutes. Remove to colander. Return water to a boil. Add scallops; cook over medium heat 3 to 4 minutes or until opaque. Remove to colander.

3. Heat oil in wok or large skillet over medium-high heat. Add jalapeño peppers; stir-fry 3 minutes. Add garlic; stir-fry 2 minutes or until garlic is fragrant and peppers are tender.

4. Stir cornstarch mixture; add to wok. Cook and stir until thickened. Add seafood, peanuts and green onions; cook and stir 2 to 3 minutes or until heated through. Stir in basil. Serve with rice.   *Makes 4 servings*

vegetables
& more

chinese sweet and sour vegetables

3 cups broccoli florets
2 medium carrots, diagonally sliced
1 large red bell pepper, cut into short, thin strips
¼ cup water
2 teaspoons cornstarch
1 teaspoon sugar
⅓ cup unsweetened pineapple juice
1 tablespoon rice vinegar
1 tablespoon soy sauce
½ teaspoon dark sesame oil
¼ cup chopped fresh cilantro (optional)

1. Combine broccoli, carrots and bell pepper in large skillet with tight-fitting lid. Add water; bring to a boil over high heat. Reduce heat to medium; cover and steam 4 minutes or until vegetables are crisp-tender. Transfer vegetables to colander; drain.

2. Meanwhile, combine cornstarch and sugar in small bowl. Stir in pineapple juice, vinegar and soy sauce until smooth; add to skillet. Cook and stir 2 minutes or until sauce boils and thickens.

3. Return vegetables to skillet; toss with sauce. Stir in sesame oil. Garnish with cilantro. *Makes 4 servings*

vegetables
& more

soba stir-fry

8 ounces uncooked soba (buckwheat) noodles or whole wheat spaghetti

½ cup reduced-sodium chicken broth

2 tablespoons reduced-sodium soy sauce

1 tablespoon dry sherry

2 teaspoons cornstarch

1 tablespoon peanut oil

2 cups sliced shiitake mushrooms

1 medium red bell pepper, cut into thin strips

2 whole dried red chiles *or* ¼ teaspoon red pepper flakes

1 clove garlic, minced

2 cups shredded napa cabbage

1 package (14 ounces) firm tofu, drained and cut into 1-inch cubes

2 green onions, thinly sliced

1. Cook noodles according to package directions. Drain and set aside.

2. Stir broth, soy sauce and sherry into cornstarch in small bowl until smooth; set aside.

3. Heat oil in wok or large nonstick skillet over medium heat. Add mushrooms, bell pepper, dried chiles and garlic; stir-fry 3 minutes or until mushrooms are tender. Add cabbage; cover and cook 2 minutes or until cabbage is wilted.

4. Stir cornstarch mixture; add to wok. Cook and stir 2 minutes or until sauce is thickened. Stir in tofu and noodles; toss gently until heated through. Sprinkle with green onions. Serve immediately.

Makes 4 servings

soba stir-fry

tofu and snow pea noodle bowl

   5 cups vegetable or chicken broth
   4 ounces uncooked vermicelli, broken in thirds
   ½ pound firm tofu, rinsed, patted dry and cut in ¼-inch cubes
   3 ounces snow peas, whole or slivered
   1 cup matchstick-size carrot strips or shredded carrots
   ½ teaspoon chili garlic sauce
   ½ cup chopped green onions
   ¼ cup chopped fresh cilantro (optional)
   2 tablespoons lime juice
   1 tablespoon grated fresh ginger
   2 teaspoons soy sauce

1. Bring broth to a boil in large saucepan over high heat. Stir in vermicelli; return to a boil. Reduce heat to medium-high; simmer 6 minutes. Stir in tofu, snow peas, carrots and chili garlic sauce; simmer 2 minutes.

2. Remove from heat; stir in green onions, cilantro, if desired, lime juice, ginger and soy sauce. Serve immediately.

Makes 4 servings

hong kong fried rice cakes

1 package (about 7 ounces) chicken-flavored rice and vermicelli mix
2 eggs, beaten
½ cup sliced green onions
2 tablespoons chopped fresh parsley
1 tablespoon hoisin sauce
1 tablespoon soy sauce
1 teaspoon minced fresh ginger
1 clove garlic, minced
2 to 3 tablespoons vegetable oil, divided

1. Prepare rice according to package directions, omitting butter. Cover and refrigerate 1 hour or until completely chilled. Add eggs, green onions, parsley, hoisin sauce, soy sauce, ginger and garlic; mix well. Form rice mixture into 3-inch cakes.

2. Heat 1 tablespoon oil in large skillet over medium heat. Cook 4 cakes at a time 3 to 4 minutes on each side or until golden brown. Add additional oil to skillet as needed. *Makes 4 to 6 servings*

marinated cucumbers

1 large cucumber (about 12 ounces)
2 tablespoons rice vinegar
2 tablespoons peanut or vegetable oil
2 tablespoons soy sauce
1½ teaspoons sugar
1 clove garlic, minced
¼ teaspoon red pepper flakes

1. Score cucumber lengthwise with tines of fork. Cut in half lengthwise; scrape out and discard seeds. Cut crosswise into ⅛-inch slices; place in medium bowl.

2. Combine remaining ingredients in small bowl; pour over cucumber and toss to coat. Cover and refrigerate at least 4 hours or up to 2 days. *Makes 4 to 6 servings*

hong kong fried rice cakes

spicy peanut noodle salad

⅓ cup *French's*® Honey Dijon Mustard
⅓ cup reduced-sodium chicken broth
⅓ cup peanut butter
2 tablespoons reduced-sodium teriyaki sauce
2 tablespoons *Frank's*® *RedHot*® Cayenne Pepper Sauce, or more to taste
2 cups thinly sliced vegetables, such as green onion, snow peas, cucumber or bell peppers
4 ounces thin spaghetti, cooked and drained (1½ cups cooked)

1. Combine mustard, chicken broth, peanut butter, teriyaki sauce and *Frank's*® *RedHot*® Sauce in large bowl; whisk until blended.

2. Add remaining ingredients; toss to coat. Serve immediately. If desired, serve on salad greens.

Makes 4 servings

szechuan eggplant

2 tablespoons peanut or vegetable oil
1 pound Asian eggplants or regular eggplant, peeled and cut into 2×½-inch strips
2 cloves garlic, minced
¼ teaspoon red pepper flakes *or* ½ teaspoon hot chili oil
¼ cup chicken broth
¼ cup hoisin sauce
3 green onions, cut into 1-inch pieces
Toasted sesame seeds*

*To toast sesame seeds, spread seeds in small skillet. Shake skillet over medium-low heat 3 minutes or until seeds begin to pop and turn golden.

1. Heat wok or large nonstick skillet over medium-high heat. Add peanut oil; heat 30 seconds. Add eggplant, garlic and red pepper flakes; stir-fry 7 minutes or until eggplant is very tender and browned.

2. Reduce heat to medium. Add broth, hoisin sauce and green onions to wok; cook 2 minutes. Sprinkle with sesame seeds.

Makes 4 to 6 servings

spicy peanut noodle salad

mongolian vegetables

1 package (about 12 ounces) firm tofu, drained
4 tablespoons soy sauce, divided
1 tablespoon dark sesame oil
1 large head bok choy (about 1½ pounds)
2 teaspoons cornstarch
1 tablespoon peanut or vegetable oil
1 large red or yellow bell pepper, cut into short, thin strips
2 cloves garlic, minced
4 green onions, cut into ½-inch pieces
2 teaspoons sesame seeds, toasted*

*To toast sesame seeds, spread seeds in small skillet. Shake skillet over medium-low heat 3 minutes or until seeds begin to pop and turn golden.

1. Press tofu lightly between paper towels; cut into ¾-inch squares or triangles. Place in shallow dish. Combine 2 tablespoons soy sauce and sesame oil; drizzle over tofu. Let stand while preparing vegetables.

2. Cut stems from bok choy leaves; cut stems into ½-inch pieces. Cut leaves crosswise into ½-inch slices.

3. Stir remaining 2 tablespoons soy sauce into cornstarch in small bowl until smooth; set aside.

4. Heat peanut oil in wok or large skillet over medium-high heat. Add bok choy stems, bell pepper and garlic; stir-fry 5 minutes. Add bok choy leaves and green onions; stir-fry 2 minutes.

5. Stir cornstarch mixture; add to wok with tofu mixture. Stir-fry 30 seconds or until sauce boils and thickens. Sprinkle with sesame seeds.

Makes 2 to 4 servings

orange-ginger tofu & noodles

⅔ cup orange juice

3 tablespoons reduced-sodium soy sauce

1 clove garlic, minced

½ to 1 teaspoon minced fresh ginger

¼ teaspoon red pepper flakes

5 ounces extra-firm tofu, well drained and cut into ½-inch cubes

1½ teaspoons cornstarch

1 teaspoon canola or peanut oil

2 cups fresh cut-up vegetables, such as broccoli, carrots, onion and snow peas

1½ cups hot cooked spaghetti or thin rice noodles

1. Combine orange juice, soy sauce, garlic, ginger and red pepper flakes in resealable food storage bag; add tofu. Marinate 20 to 30 minutes. Drain tofu,* reserving marinade. Stir marinade into cornstarch in small bowl until smooth; set aside.

2. Heat oil in wok or large nonstick skillet over medium-high heat. Add vegetables; stir-fry 2 to 3 minutes or until vegetables are crisp-tender. Add tofu; stir-fry 1 minute. Stir cornstarch mixture; add to wok. Bring to a boil; boil 1 minute. Serve over noodles. *Makes 2 servings*

*Tofu must be drained before being stir-fried. Remove any remaining liquid by placing the block of tofu on several layers of paper towels and covering it with additional paper towels weighted down with a heavy plate. Let stand for 15 to 20 minutes.

orange-ginger tofu & noodles

easy fried rice

¼ cup BERTOLLI® Olive Oil
4 cups cooked rice
2 cloves garlic, finely chopped
1 envelope LIPTON® RECIPE SECRETS® Onion Mushroom Soup Mix
½ cup water
1 tablespoon soy sauce
1 cup frozen peas and carrots, partially thawed
2 eggs, lightly beaten

1. In 12-inch nonstick skillet, heat olive oil over medium-high heat and cook rice, stirring constantly, 2 minutes or until rice is heated through. Stir in garlic.

2. Stir in soup mix blended with water and soy sauce and cook 1 minute. Stir in peas and carrots and cook 2 minutes or until heated through.

3. Make a well in center of rice and quickly stir in eggs until cooked.   *Makes 4 servings*

stir-fried spinach with garlic

2 teaspoons peanut or vegetable oil
1 clove garlic, minced
6 cups packed torn stemmed spinach (about 8 ounces)
2 teaspoons soy sauce
1 teaspoon rice vinegar
¼ teaspoon sugar
1 teaspoon toasted sesame seeds

1. Heat wok or large skillet over medium-high heat. Add oil; heat 30 seconds. Add garlic; stir-fry 1 minute.

2. Add spinach, soy sauce, vinegar and sugar; stir-fry 1 to 2 minutes until spinach is wilted. Sprinkle with sesame seeds.   *Makes 2 servings*

easy fried rice

rice noodles with broccoli and tofu

1 package (14 ounces) firm or extra-firm tofu
1 package (8 to 10 ounces) wide rice noodles
2 tablespoons peanut oil
3 shallots, sliced
6 cloves garlic, minced
1 jalapeño pepper,* minced
2 teaspoons minced fresh ginger
3 cups broccoli florets
¼ cup soy sauce
1 to 2 tablespoons fish sauce
  Fresh basil leaves (optional)

*Jalapeño peppers can sting and irritate the skin, so wear rubber gloves when handling peppers and do not touch your eyes.

1. Cut tofu crosswise into 2 pieces, each about 1 inch thick. Place tofu on cutting board between layers of paper towels; place another cutting board on top to add weight to press moisture out of tofu. Soak rice noodles in large bowl filled with boiling water; let stand 30 minutes or until soft.

2. Cut tofu into bite-sized squares and blot dry. Heat oil in wok or large skillet. Add tofu to wok; stir-fry about 5 minutes or until tofu is lightly browned on all sides. Remove from wok.

3. Add shallots, garlic, jalapeño pepper and ginger to wok; stir-fry over medium-high heat 2 to 3 minutes. Add broccoli; stir-fry 1 minute. Cover and cook 3 minutes or until broccoli is crisp-tender.

4. Drain noodles well; stir into wok. Return tofu to wok. Add soy sauce and fish sauce; stir-fry 8 minutes or until noodles are coated and flavors are blended. Garnish with basil. *Makes 4 to 6 servings*

rice noodles with broccoli and tofu

spinach and mushroom stir-fry

2 tablespoons peanut oil
2 cloves garlic, minced
1 teaspoon minced fresh ginger
¼ to ½ teaspoon red pepper flakes
1 red bell pepper, cut into 1-inch triangles
2 ounces shiitake or button mushrooms,* sliced
10 ounces spinach, washed, stemmed and coarsely chopped
1 teaspoon fish sauce

*Or, substitute ½-ounce dried shiitake mushrooms, soaked according to package directions.

1. Heat wok over high heat 1 minute. Drizzle oil into wok; heat 30 seconds. Add garlic, ginger and red pepper flakes; stir-fry 30 seconds.

2. Add bell pepper and mushrooms to wok; stir-fry 2 minutes. Add spinach and fish sauce; stir-fry 1 to 2 minutes or until spinach is wilted.

Makes 4 servings

 tip | Shiitake mushrooms are large, dark brown mushrooms with a rich, smoky flavor and woodsy aroma. They have dense, meaty flesh and tough, woody stems that should be removed before cooking.

vegetarian asian noodles with peanut sauce

½ package (about 9 ounces) uncooked udon noodles* *or*
    4 ounces uncooked whole wheat spaghetti
1 tablespoon vegetable oil
2 cups snow peas, cut diagonally into bite-size pieces
1 cup shredded carrots
¼ cup chopped green onions
¼ cup hot water
¼ cup peanut butter
2 to 4 tablespoons chili garlic sauce
1 tablespoon soy sauce
¼ cup dry-roasted peanuts

*Udon noodles, wheat flour noodles, are usually available in the Asian section of natural food stores or in larger supermarkets.

1. Cook noodles according to package directions. Drain; keep warm.

2. Meanwhile, heat oil in wok or large skillet over medium-high heat. Add snow peas and carrots; stir-fry 2 minutes. Remove from heat.

3. Add greens onions, water, peanut butter, chili garlic sauce and soy sauce to wok; mix well. Stir in noodles; toss to coat. Sprinkle with peanuts. Serve warm or at room temperature.   *Makes 4 servings*

Tip: To save time, use packaged shredded carrots.

vegetarian asian noodles
with peanut sauce

fried tofu with asian vegetables

  1 pound firm tofu
½ cup reduced-sodium soy sauce, divided
  1 cup all-purpose flour
¾ teaspoon salt, divided
⅛ teaspoon pepper
   Vegetable oil for frying
  2 packages (16 ounces each) frozen mixed Asian vegetables*
  3 tablespoons water
  1 teaspoon cornstarch
  3 tablespoons plum sauce
  2 tablespoons lemon juice
  2 teaspoons sugar
  1 teaspoon minced fresh ginger
⅛ to ¼ teaspoon red pepper flakes

*Frozen vegetables do not need to be thawed before cooking.

1. Drain tofu; cut into ¾-inch cubes. Gently mix tofu and ¼ cup soy sauce in shallow bowl; let stand 5 minutes. Combine flour, ½ teaspoon salt and pepper on plate. Gently toss tofu cubes, a small amount at a time, with flour mixture to coat.

2. Heat 1½ inches oil in Dutch oven or wok. Test heat by dropping one tofu cube into oil. It should brown in 1 minute. Fry tofu cubes in small batches until browned. Remove from oil with slotted spoon; drain on paper towels.

3. Pour off all but 1 tablespoon oil from Dutch oven. Add frozen vegetables and remaining ¼ teaspoon salt. Cook over medium-high heat 6 minutes, stirring occasionally, or until vegetables are heated through. Increase heat to high to evaporate any remaining liquid. Set aside and cover to keep warm.

4. Stir water into cornstarch in small bowl until smooth. Combine cornstarch mixture, remaining ¼ cup soy sauce, plum sauce, lemon juice, sugar, ginger and red pepper flakes in small saucepan; cook and stir over low heat 1 to 2 minutes or until sauce is slightly thickened.

5. Spoon vegetables into serving bowl. Top with tofu and sauce; toss gently to mix.   *Makes 6 servings*

szechuan vegetable lo mein

2 cans (about 14 ounces each) vegetable or chicken broth

2 teaspoons minced garlic

1 teaspoon minced fresh ginger

¼ teaspoon red pepper flakes

1 package (16 ounces) frozen vegetable medley, such as broccoli, carrots, water chestnuts and red bell peppers

1 package (5 ounces) ramen noodles or 5 ounces uncooked angel hair pasta, broken in half

3 tablespoons soy sauce

1 tablespoon dark sesame oil

¼ cup thinly sliced green onions

1. Combine broth, garlic, ginger and red pepper flakes in large deep skillet. Cover and bring to a boil over high heat.

2. Add vegetables and noodles to skillet; cover and return to a boil. Reduce heat to medium-low; simmer, uncovered, 5 to 6 minutes or until vegetables and noodles are tender, stirring occasionally.

3. Stir in soy sauce and sesame oil; cook 3 minutes. Stir in green onions.

Makes 4 servings

Note: For a heartier, protein-packed main dish, add 1 package (10½ ounces) extra-firm tofu, cut into ¾-inch pieces, to the broth mixture with the soy sauce and sesame oil.

curried noodles

7 ounces dried Chinese rice sticks or rice noodles
1 tablespoon peanut or vegetable oil
1 large red bell pepper, cut into short, thin strips
2 green onions, cut into ½-inch pieces
1 clove garlic, minced
1 teaspoon minced fresh ginger
2 teaspoons curry powder
⅛ to ¼ teaspoon red pepper flakes
½ cup chicken broth
2 tablespoons soy sauce

1. Place rice sticks in bowl; cover with boiling water. Soak 15 minutes to soften. Drain and cut into 3-inch pieces.

2. Heat wok or large skillet over medium-high heat. Add oil; heat 30 seconds. Add bell pepper; stir-fry 3 minutes. Add green onions, garlic and ginger; stir-fry 1 minute. Add curry powder and red pepper flakes; stir-fry 1 minute.

3. Add broth and soy sauce; cook and stir 2 minutes. Add noodles; cook 3 minutes or until heated through.

Makes 6 servings

 tip | Rice-flour noodles are available in a variety of different thicknesses, ranging from as thin as angel hair pasta up to about 1 inch wide. The term "rice sticks" is most often applied to flat rice noodles about ¼ inch wide that are commonly used in soups and stir-fries. All rice noodles must be soaked in hot or boiling water before using unless they will be fried. They are becoming increasingly availabe in large supermarkets, or shop in Asian markets for the best selection.

curried noodles

dragon tofu

¼ **cup soy sauce**

 1 **tablespoon creamy peanut butter**

 1 **package (about 12 ounces) firm tofu, drained**

 1 **medium zucchini**

 1 **medium yellow squash**

 2 **teaspoons peanut or vegetable oil**

½ **teaspoon hot chili oil**

 2 **cloves garlic, minced**

 2 **cups (packed) torn spinach leaves**

¼ **cup coarsely chopped cashews or peanuts (optional)**

1. Whisk soy sauce and peanut butter in small bowl until well blended. Press tofu lightly between paper towels; cut into ¾-inch squares or triangles. Place in single layer in shallow dish. Pour soy sauce mixture over tofu; stir gently to coat all surfaces. Let stand at room temperature 20 minutes.

2. Cut zucchini and yellow squash lengthwise into ¼-inch-thick slices; cut each slice into 2×¼-inch strips.

3. Heat peanut and chili oils in large nonstick skillet over medium-high heat. Add zucchini, yellow squash and garlic; stir-fry 3 minutes. Add tofu mixture; cook 2 minutes or until tofu is heated through and sauce is slightly thickened, stirring occasionally. Stir in spinach; remove from heat. Sprinkle with cashews, if desired.

Makes 2 servings

The publisher would like to thank the companies listed below for the use of their recipes and photographs in this publication.

ACH Food Companies, Inc.

Hormel Foods, LLC

Lee Kum Kee (USA) Inc.

MASTERFOODS USA

National Pork Board

Reckitt Benckiser Inc.

Unilever

USA Rice Federation[TM]

acknowledgments

155

index

VOLUME MEASUREMENTS (dry)

¹⁄₈ teaspoon = 0.5 mL
¹⁄₄ teaspoon = 1 mL
¹⁄₂ teaspoon = 2 mL
³⁄₄ teaspoon = 4 mL
1 teaspoon = 5 mL
1 tablespoon = 15 mL
2 tablespoons = 30 mL
¹⁄₄ cup = 60 mL
¹⁄₃ cup = 75 mL
¹⁄₂ cup = 125 mL
²⁄₃ cup = 150 mL
³⁄₄ cup = 175 mL
1 cup = 250 mL
2 cups = 1 pint = 500 mL
3 cups = 750 mL
4 cups = 1 quart = 1 L

VOLUME MEASUREMENTS (fluid)

1 fluid ounce (2 tablespoons) = 30 mL
4 fluid ounces (¹⁄₂ cup) = 125 mL
8 fluid ounces (1 cup) = 250 mL
12 fluid ounces (1¹⁄₂ cups) = 375 mL
16 fluid ounces (2 cups) = 500 mL

WEIGHTS (mass)

¹⁄₂ ounce = 15 g
1 ounce = 30 g
3 ounces = 90 g
4 ounces = 120 g
8 ounces = 225 g
10 ounces = 285 g
12 ounces = 360 g
16 ounces = 1 pound = 450 g

DIMENSIONS

¹⁄₁₆ inch = 2 mm
¹⁄₈ inch = 3 mm
¹⁄₄ inch = 6 mm
¹⁄₂ inch = 1.5 cm
³⁄₄ inch = 2 cm
1 inch = 2.5 cm

OVEN TEMPERATURES

250°F = 120°C
275°F = 140°C
300°F = 150°C
325°F = 160°C
350°F = 180°C
375°F = 190°C
400°F = 200°C
425°F = 220°C
450°F = 230°C

BAKING PAN SIZES

Utensil	Size in Inches/Quarts	Metric Volume	Size in Centimeters
Baking or Cake Pan (square or rectangular)	8×8×2	2 L	20×20×5
	9×9×2	2.5 L	23×23×5
	12×8×2	3 L	30×20×5
	13×9×2	3.5 L	33×23×5
Loaf Pan	8×4×3	1.5 L	20×10×7
	9×5×3	2 L	23×13×7
Round Layer Cake Pan	8×1½	1.2 L	20×4
	9×1½	1.5 L	23×4
Pie Plate	8×1¼	750 mL	20×3
	9×1¼	1 L	23×3
Baking Dish or Casserole	1 quart	1 L	—
	1½ quart	1.5 L	—
	2 quart	2 L	—

metric conversion chart